First published in Great Britain in 2006 by HarperCollins Children's Books.
HarperCollins Children's Books is a division of HarperCollins Publishers Ltd.
The HarperCollins Children's Books website is www.harpercollinschildrensbooks.co.uk

1 3 5 7 9 10 8 6 4 2

© The Football Association Limited 2006

The FA Crest and The FA England Crest are official trade marks of The Football Association Limited
and are subject of extensive trade mark registrations worldwide.

Photographs © Empics/PA 2006

Correct at time of printing March 2006

TheFA.com

Text by Richard Mead

ISBN: 0-00-721697-1

A CIP catalogue for this title is available from the British Library. All rights reserved. No part of this publication may be reproduced, stored in a retrieval system or transmitted in any form or by any means, electronic, mechanical, photocopying, recording or otherwise, without the prior permission of HarperCollins Publishers Ltd, 77 - 85 Fulham Palace Road, Hammersmith, London W6 8JB.

The HarperCollins website address is www.harpercollinschildrensbooks.co.uk

Printed and bound in Great Britain by Clays Ltd, St Ives plc

ENGLAND
QUIZ AND JOKE BOOK

HarperCollins *Children's Books*

Game On!

Are you ready for Germany 2006? Billions of football fans are counting down the days to the world's biggest sporting event. More people will follow the nail-biting excitement of this World Cup than watch the Olympic Games!

32 teams are coming together at the tournament, all hoping to claim the trophy. Host nation Germany, two time winners Argentina and South Korea, who memorably reached the semi-finals in 2002, are just some of the sides hoping 2006 will be their year. But they'll have to stop England first...

That's going to be a tough task with world-class stars such as David Beckham, Michael Owen, Rio Ferdinand, John Terry, Frank Lampard, Ashley Cole, Wayne Rooney and Steven Gerrard in the squad. And as it's exactly 40 years ago that England won the World Cup, 2006 is the perfect time to bring the trophy back home!

If you can't wait for all that fantastic footie to begin, you've come to the right place. This book is crammed with puzzles and quizzes about the famous '66 team, the current England squad and every single World Cup tournament. There are also amazing stories from past finals – and jokes to cheer you up if any of the results don't go the right way!

So read on and get ready to cheer England all the way to World Cup glory...

The Kicking Contents

PAGE 8 **WORLD CUP CHALLENGES – FIRST HALF**
Quizzes on every World Cup from Uruguay '30 to West Germany '74 plus picture puzzles and mystery players to identify.

PAGE 38 **FOOTIE FUNNIES**
Packed with puns from Knock Knock! jokes to shaggy dog stories, these gags are guaranteed to make you giggle.

PAGE 68 **TOURNAMENT TALES**
A royal pitch invasion, shorts that don't stay up, a doggie detective and a match that ended 31-0! You can read all about it here.

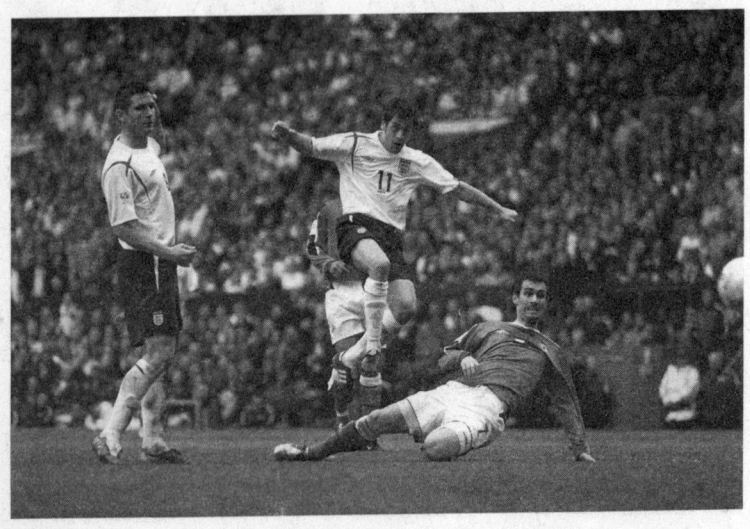

PAGE 78 ENGLAND ENIGMAS
Wordsearches, anagrams, spot the ball and lots more... not forgetting some fiendish quiz questions on England's World Cup teams.

PAGE 108 WORLD CUP CHALLENGES – SECOND HALF
Get bang up to date and test your knowledge on all the tournaments from Argentina '78 to Germany '06 and find the World Cup record breakers.

PAGE 128 ALL THE ANSWERS
Don't be left feeling flummoxed! Check your answers here to find out how much you really know...

World Cup Challenges - First Half

Are you a World Cup winner or a finals flop?
Test your knowledge with these tricky teasers and puzzles.

CUP CLASSICS
In this book you'll find five fiendish quizzes on every single World Cup tournament. But first it's time to show your soccer skill with these ten toughies! They cover all the tournaments from Uruguay in 1930 to Japan and South Korea in 2002.

1. Brazil has won the World Cup more often than any other team. How many times have they been champions?
    a) Three
    b) Four
    c) Five
    d) Six

2. No team has appeared in every World Cup finals but Brazil have come closest, only missing one tournament. True or false?

3. What links Sándor Kocsis (Hungary), Just Fontaine (France), Gerd Müller (West Germany) and Gabriel Batistuta (Argentina)?
    a) They've each scored three own goals at World Cup finals
    b) They've each scored two hat tricks in World Cup finals
    c) They've each been sent off in two different games in one

tournament
d) They've each scored the winning goal in a World Cup final

TOUGH TO TACKLE...
4. How many times has the host nation won the World Cup?

5. The World Cup has been held every four years since the first tournament in 1930 – true or false?

6. Which team have been World Cup runners-up more times than any other country?
   a) Argentina
   b) Brazil
   c) Italy
   d) West Germany

7. In which World Cup tournament were the most goals scored?
   a) Italy '90
   b) USA '94
   c) France '98
   d) Japan and South Korea '02

8. Since the first tournament in 1930 just seven countries have won the World Cup – true or false?

9. Frenchman Abel Lafleur and Italian Silvio Gazzarriga have both had their hands on the World Cup. How?
   a) They each managed World Cup winning teams

b) They were both caught trying to steal the trophy
c) They each designed a World Cup trophy
d) They are security guards hired by FIFA to accompany the trophy whenever it is put on display

10. Which football team did World Cup superstars Pelé, Bobby Moore and Ossie Ardiles all play for?

Boot-iful Goals

The Golden Boot is awarded to the player who scores the most goals at each World Cup. All the footballers listed below were tournament top scorers but the dates and the players' nationalities have got mixed up. Can you put them in the correct order?

PLAYERS	COUNTRY	TOURNAMENT
Eusebio – 9 goals	Argentina	1998
	....	
Mario Kempes – 6 goals	Brazil	1986
	....	
Sándor Kocsis – 11 goals	Croatia	1978
	....	
Leonidas – 8 goals	England	1966
	....	
Gary Lineker – 6 goals	Hungary	1954
	....	
Davor Suker – 6 goals	Portugal	1938
	....	

Uruguay '30 Quick Quiz

WINNERS URUGUAY

1. Just 13 teams competed in the first World Cup in 1930. Which one of these countries took part?
    a) Belgium
    b) Colombia
    c) Italy
    d) Nigeria

2. The host nation, Uruguay, had won the football gold medal at the 1924 and 1928 Olympics. True or false?

3. Who selected the players for the Romanian team?
    a) The Romanian people in a national vote
    b) The country's monarch, King Carol
    c) FIFA, the organisers of the World Cup
    d) A panel of Romanian army officers

4. Why did Uruguay have their first game delayed until five days after the tournament began?
    a) Most of their players were suffering with food poisoning
    b) FIFA rules stated the host nation had to wait until all the other teams had played their first round matches
    c) Their new stadium was still being built
    d) The tickets had been printed with the wrong date and so the match was rescheduled

TOUGH TO TACKLE...

5. The date of the first ever World Cup goal was 13th July 1930. Which team were the first to find the back of the net?

Italy '34 Quick Quiz

WINNERS ITALY

1. In 1934 Mexico travelled to Italy but didn't take part in the World Cup finals. Why not?

    a) The team was banned because of the players' behaviour on the journey to Italy
    b) They didn't play their final World Cup qualifying game until they were in Rome – and they lost!
    c) They'd come as spectators, hoping to pick up tips for qualifying in 1938
    d) The team withdrew after the Italian newspapers called the players cheats

2. Although the competition was being held in Italy, the Italian team still had to qualify for the competition by playing Greece. True or false?

3. The quarter-final between Italy and Spain ended in a 1-1 draw after extra time. How was it decided?
    a) A penalty shoot-out
    b) A rematch – the next day
    c) The referee tossed a coin
    d) Spain went through because they scored the first goal

TOUGH TO TACKLE...

4. At which stage did the World Cup holders Uruguay get

knocked out in 1934?

5. Italy won the final but needed extra time to do it. Which team did they beat?
   a) Argentina
   b) Brazil
   c) Czechoslovakia
   d) Holland

Mystery Manager

The clues below will help you reveal the identity of a famous World Cup player and manager. How quickly can you identify him?

1. He was born on 11th September 1945.

2. He began his League career on the left wing but soon switched to his famous role of attacking sweeper.

3. His first World Cup tournament was in 1966 – he played in the final.

4. In the 1970 tournament he played in the semi-final with his arm in a sling!

5. He is only one of only two players to have won a complete collection of World Cup medals – gold, silver and bronze.

6. His gold medal came at the 1974 game when he led his team, West Germany, to victory.

7. German fans nicknamed him the Kaiser, which means the Emperor.

8. When West Germany won the World Cup in 1990, he was the team's manager, becoming the second man to captain and coach a World Cup winning team.

Find the Ball

Here's some top action from the 2002 World Cup final when Brazil beat Germany 2-0. But there's one thing missing – the ball! Which grid square has it been removed from?

France '38 Quick Quiz

WINNERS ITALY

TOUGH TO TACKLE...

1. Cuba made their first finals appearance in 1938. Their qualifying group contained Colombia, Costa Rica, Mexico, El Salvador and Surinam. How many matches did Cuba have to play to qualify for France '38?

2. The first round game between Brazil and Poland was a classic match. How many goals were scored?
   a) Five
   b) Seven
   c) Nine
   d) 11

3. In the Brazil versus Poland game, striker Leonidas scored a hat trick in the first half. He tried to play the second half without part of his kit – what had he taken off?
   a) Shirt
   b) Shorts
   c) Socks
   d) Boots

4. Why did Sweden not play a first round match and instead receive a bye into the quarter-finals?
   a) At the last minute, it was realised that only 15 teams had been invited to the finals

b) Austria had qualified but were forced to withdraw after the country was invaded by Germany
c) It was an apology by FIFA for not choosing Sweden to host the competition
d) Their first round opponents, Argentina, were stuck in the Atlantic Ocean on a very slow boat

5. Apart from the goalkeeper, the Italian side that won the 1938 World Cup final was the same one that collected the trophy in 1934. True or false?

Brazil '50 Quick Quiz

WINNERS URUGUAY

1. Only 13 teams turned up for the 1950 World Cup. Scotland were one of the teams who qualified but they refused to go. Why?
    a) They finished second in their qualifying group and refused to go because they were runners-up
    b) They thought the competition should take place in Britain, especially as it been held in South America before
    c) The competition clashed with the Scottish FA Cup final and Scotland refused to send a team unless FIFA delayed the World Cup by a week
    d) The entire Scotland team went on strike, demanding higher wages

2. Brazil and Uruguay both got through to the second round but Brazil had to play three first round matches and Uruguay only had to play one. True or false?

3. The crowd that watched Brazil take on Uruguay at the Maracana Stadium set a world record for the largest football attendance. How many people watched the game?
    a) 125,354
    b) 164,297
    c) 199,854
    d) 242,987

4. Although Uruguay won the trophy, there was no official World Cup final match. True or false?

TOUGH TO TACKLE...

5. Which team scored the most goals in the 1950 World Cup?

Switzerland '54 Quick Quiz

WINNERS WEST GERMANY

1. In the first round, the teams were divided up into four leagues each containing four teams. So why did each team only play two games?
   a) After two games, the top two teams in all the leagues couldn't be caught by the bottom teams so it was decided to move on to the next round
   b) Freak snowstorms caused havoc with the schedule and there wasn't time for any more games
   c) Two teams in each group were seeded by FIFA and it was decided the top two teams wouldn't play each other and neither would the bottom two
   d) After an argument about prize money, Mexico, Turkey, Czechoslovakia and Belgium withdrew after the opening ceremony leaving three teams in each group

2. One match played at Berne Stadium was later called the Battle of Berne! Three players were sent off and after the game there was a huge fight in the dressing room. Which two teams were involved?
   a) Austria and Switzerland
   b) Hungary and Brazil
   c) West Germany and Yugoslavia
   d) Uruguay and England

3. When Uruguay's Juan Eduardo Hohberg scored against Hungary, an unusual goal celebration followed. The team

formed a human pyramid with Hohberg standing at the top – true or false?

4. Which of these teams lost their first ever World Cup game at this tournament?
   a) Brazil
   b) Italy
   c) Peru
   d) Uruguay

TOUGH TO TACKLE...
5. West Germany won the World Cup by beating Hungary 3-2. But which team thrashed West Germany 8-3 in the first round of the tournament?

Host Nations

Places, everyone! Fit the names of the World Cup host nations from 1930 to 2006 in the grid below, ignoring the spaces in WEST GERMANY and SOUTH KOREA.

- URUGUAY
- ITALY
- FRANCE
- BRAZIL
- SWITZERLAND
- SWEDEN
- CHILE
- ENGLAND
- MEXICO
- WEST GERMANY
- ARGENTINA
- SPAIN
- USA
- JAPAN
- SOUTH KOREA
- GERMANY

Face Off!

Can you identify which two current England players have been merged in the picture below?

Sweden '58 Quick Quiz

WINNERS BRAZIL

1. England, Scotland, Wales and Northern Ireland all qualified for the 1958 World Cup finals – the only time this has happened. True or false?

2. Which country appeared in Sweden after winning the Asia and Africa qualifying group?
   a) China
   b) Israel
   c) Turkey
   d) Wales

3. At the end of the first round, so many teams were level on points that all four groups had to be settled by play-off games. True or false?

4. This was Pelé's first appearance at a World Cup finals. How many goals did he score in the tournament?
    a) 0
    b) 2
    c) 4
    d) 6

TOUGH TO TACKLE...

5. Brazil played six games on their way to collecting the World Cup and won five of them. Which team did they fail to beat?

Chile '62 Quick Quiz

WINNERS BRAZIL

1. Which South American team reached the World Cup finals for the first time in 1962?
   a) Colombia
   b) Ecuador
   c) Peru
   d) Venezuela

2. The first round game between Chile and Italy was a bad-tempered match. When Italy's Giorgio Ferrini was sent off, how long did it take him to leave the pitch?
   a) Two minutes
   b) Five minutes
   c) Eight minutes
   d) He refused to go and sat by the goalpost for the rest of the game

3. Bulgaria were the only team to lose all three of their first round matches. True or false?

4. The biggest crowd for this tournament was 76,594 for the semi-final between Chile and Brazil. How many people watched the other semi-final between Czechoslovakia and Yugoslavia?
   a) 6,000
   b) 16,000
   c) 60,000
   d) 66,000

TOUGH TO TACKLE...

5. This wasn't a high-scoring tournament – no player managed to find the back of the net more than four times. How many players tied as the tournament's top-scorers?

England '66 Quick Quiz

WINNERS ENGLAND

1. After winning the World Cup in 1958 and 1962, Brazil were favourites to win again in 1966. At which stage of the finals were they eliminated?
    a) They dropped out before the tournament began
    b) First round
    c) Quarter-final
    d) Semi-final

2. Which of these was not a venue for a World Cup finals game?
    a) Old Trafford, Manchester
    c) Roker Park, Sunderland
    c) Villa Park, Birmingham
    d) White Hart Lane, London

3. Nobby Stiles was booked for a foul after England's game against France had finished! True or false?

4. North Korea played in their first finals in 1966. Their quarter-final game against mighty Portugal was a cracker, with the Asian team leading 3-0 at one point. What was the final score?
    a) North Korea 3 Portugal 0
    b) North Korea 4 Portugal 3
    c) North Korea 3 Portugal 5
    d) North Korea 5 Portugal 6

TOUGH TO TACKLE...

5. How many goals did World Cup winners England concede in their six games during the tournament?

Mascot Mania

Since 1966, every World Cup has had its own mascot. Match up each tournament with the right mascot. The first one has been done for you.

TOURNAMENT

A. England 1966 ⟵

B. Mexico 1970

C. West Germany 1974

D. Argentina 1978

E. Spain 1982

F. Mexico 1986

G. Italy 1990

H. USA 1994

I. France 1998

J. Japan and South Korea 2002

K. Germany 2006

MASCOT

1. Striker

2. Tip and Tap

3. Footix

4. Pique

⟶ 5. World Cup Willie

6. Naranjito

7. Goleo VI

8. Kaz, Ato and Nik

9. Gauchito

10. Ciao

11. Juanito

Final Foes

All these teams have appeared in at least one World Cup final. How quickly can you find them in the grid? Words can be horizontal, vertical or diagonal and forwards or backwards!

- ARGENTINA
- BRAZIL
- ENGLAND
- FRANCE
- GERMANY
- HOLLAND
- HUNGARY
- ITALY
- SWEDEN

```
N Y N A M R E G D S
F E N W I N A Y N W
Z R X T G I R S A E
X T A L D A G W L D
K L A N G R E W L E
Y N G N C Z N C O N
D J U M F E T A H E
R H B R A Z I L Z S
E T A E E S N L F S
P P P A E J A Y J J
```

Mexico '70 Quick Quiz

WINNERS BRAZIL

1. Plenty of famous teams failed to qualify for Mexico. Only one of these European countries reached the finals – which one?
   a) France
   b) Portugal
   c) Sweden
   d) Spain

2. Substitutes were allowed for the first time in a World Cup finals tournament in Mexico. True or false?

3. Why did the referee of the game between West Germany and Morocco start the second half – and then have to suddenly stop it again?
   a) The ball had gone flat and there wasn't a spare one
   b) The referee realised his watch was broken
   c) Angry West German fans had dug up part of the pitch at half time
   d) Some of the Moroccan players were still sitting in the dressing room

TOUGH TO TACKLE...

4. Jairzinho scored in the final – and set an incredible World Cup record. What was the superb striker's amazing achievement?

5. Brazil were awarded the Jules Rimet trophy to keep for winning the World Cup three times. Why isn't it currently on display?
   a) It's been stolen
   b) FIFA asked for it back in 2002
   c) It was lost during the team's journey back to Brazil
   d) It was given to Pelé when he retired from the game

West Germany '74 Quick Quiz

WINNERS WEST GERMANY

1. Several teams made their first World Cup finals appearance in West Germany. Which of these teams didn't make their debut at the 1974 tournament?
   a) Australia
   b) China
   c) Haiti
   d) Zaire

2. Red and yellow cards were issued to referees for the first time in a World Cup finals tournament in 1974. True or false?

3. One first round game saw East Germany take on West Germany. Which team won?

4. Which unlucky team became the first side in World Cup history to get knocked out of the finals without losing a game?
   a) Bulgaria
   b) Chile
   c) Italy
   d) Scotland

TOUGH TO TACKLE...

5. The 1974 final between West Germany and Holland was delayed because something was missing from the pitch. What should have been there but wasn't?

Footie Funnies

You've got to have a sense of humour to be a football fan – and this gaggle of gags and groans proves it!

POTTY PLAYERS

Why do knights make excellent centre-forwards?
Because they can shield the ball!

Why was the barber a champion footballer?
He was brilliant at doing scissor kicks!

Why was the bricklayer such a good defender?
He was terrific at building walls!

Why is it good to have an Olympic swimmer in your team?
Because he'll be ace at diving headers!

Why did the accident-prone player keep getting taller?
He was always on a stretcher!

What was the score when two teams of ballerinas played football?
A tutu draw!

Why did the layabout join his local football team?
He wanted to have a goal in life!

What does a goalkeeper have when he doesn't feel well?
Gloves on his hands!

Why was Cinderella useless at football?
She had a pumpkin for a coach – and she kept running away from the ball!

Why did Billy think he'd be great at running up the wing?
He'd just found out he'd got athlete's foot!

Why did Rovers have a potato in their team?
Because it was a crisp finisher!

Joe: Sorry I sent that penalty over the bar. I could kick myself.
Jack: I wouldn't risk it – you'd probably miss!

Why did the orange win so many free kicks?
He was always a-peel-ing to the referee!

How do ghost football players stay fit?
They exorcise a lot!

Why did the manager nickname his player 'Jigsaw'?
Because he always went to pieces in the box!

What is a star player awarded if he fails to score in a game?
A constellation prize!

Who guards the net for the spooks' football team?
The ghoulie!

When is a footballer like a grandfather clock?
When he's a striker!

What does a footballer do if he splits his sides laughing?
Runs until he gets a stitch!

Who's the tidiest player on the pitch?
The sweeper!

Manager: I don't think you'll ever be allowed to join the players' union, Kyle.
Kyle: Why not, boss?
Manager: Because you're a useless striker!

How do you stop a stinky footballer from smelling?
Put a peg on his nose!

Why did the manager have the pitch flooded?
So he could bring on a sub!

Why did the footballer take a rubber duck onto the pitch?
He was expecting an early bath!

Harry: I've got some bad news, coach. I've seen the physio and he's told me I can't play football.
Coach: So he must have seen you in Saturday's match too!

When is a footballer like a baby?
When he dribbles!

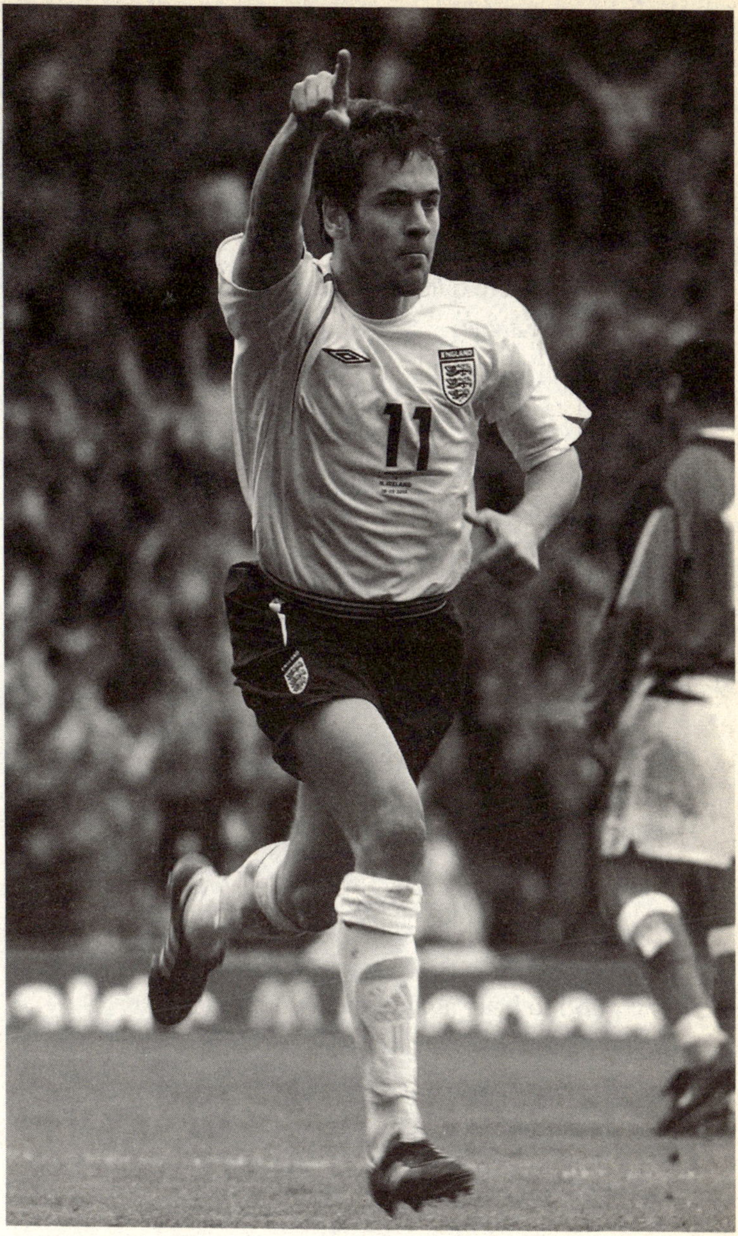

What do you call a noisy soccer player?
A foot-bawler!

What's the difference between a gutter and a poor goalie?
One catches drops but the other drops catches!

Finbar: I've got to quit playing football because of illness and fatigue.
Damien: That's dreadful. What's the problem exactly?
Finbar: The fans are sick and tired of me!

BEASTLY BEHAVIOUR

Why do centipedes make such bad footballers?
Because by the time they've put their boots on, the game is almost over!

Why is football like milk?
Because it strengthens the calves!

What do you get if you cross a footballer with a rhino?
I don't know, but I wouldn't get in its way!

Why is it good to have a monkey in your team?
Because he's good at banana shots!

How does a rabbit feel when its team loses?
Sick as a carrot!

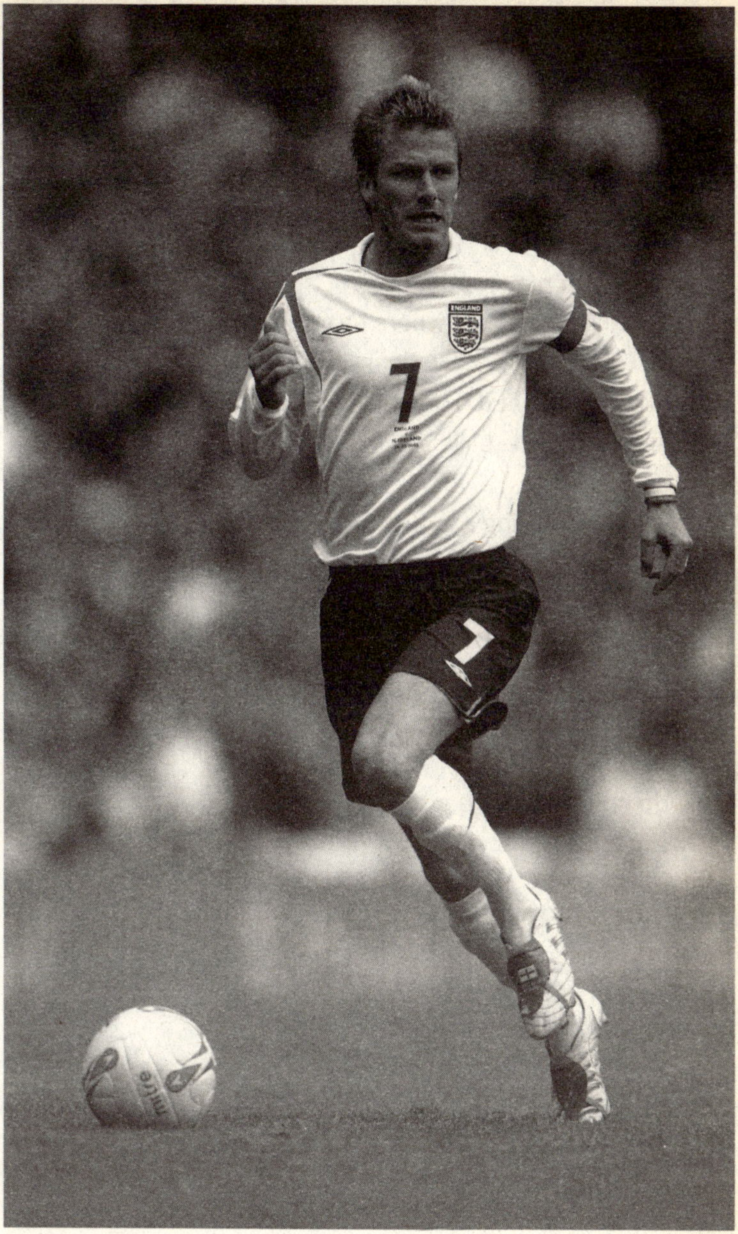
7
mitre

Why do turkeys hate playing football?
Because they're always getting stuffed!

What position do ducks play?
Right and left quack!

Why can't fish play football?
They don't like going anywhere near the net!

Why are pigs banned from playing football?
They always hog the ball!

Two flies were kicking a football around a saucer.
"We'll have to improve by next week," said one of the flies.
"We're playing in the cup!"

Why don't elephants make good footballers?
Because they've got two left feet!

How do chickens leave a football stadium?
They use the eggs-it!

TAKING THE KNOCKS!

Knock Knock!
Who's there?
Alec!
Alec who?
Alec England – they're my favourite team!

Knock Knock!
Who's there?
Alison!
Alison who?
Alison to all the match reports on my radio!

Knock Knock!
Who's there?
Anna!
Anna who?
Anna-racs keep supporters dry at matches!

Knock Knock!
Who's there?
Annette!
Annette who?
Annette is attached to the goalpost!

Knock Knock!
Who's there?
Annie!
Annie who?
Annie body going to score a goal soon?

Knock Knock!
Who's there?
Charlotte!
Charlotte who?
Charlotte of fans turned up to watch today!

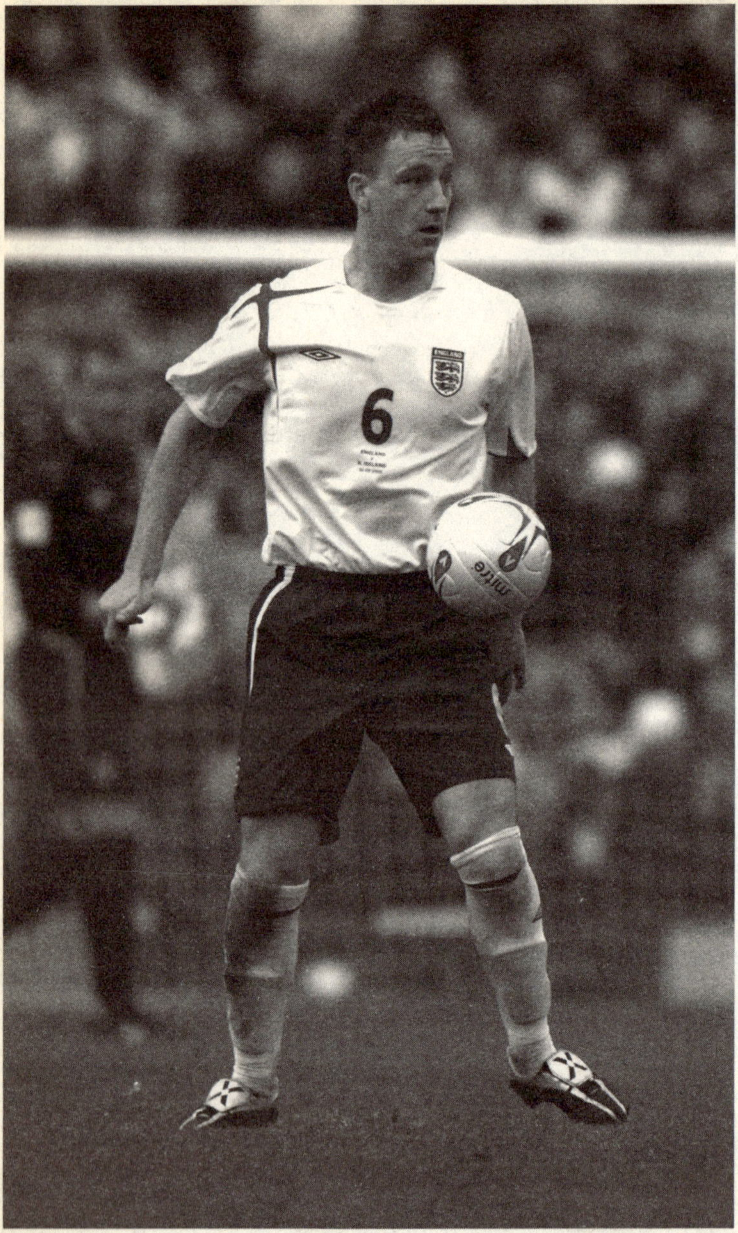
6

Knock Knock!
Who's there?
Daisy!
Daisy who?
Daisy plays football but at nights he sleeps!

Knock Knock!
Who's there?
Doris!
Doris who?
Doris locked to the changing room – let me in!

Knock Knock!
Who's there?
Godfrey!
Godfrey who?
Godfrey tickets to the World Cup final!

Knock Knock!
Who's there?
Justin!
Justin who?
Justin time for kick-off!

Knock Knock!
Who's there?
Kerry!
Kerry who?
Kerry me off the pitch – I've twisted my ankle!

Knock Knock!
Who's there?
Les!
Les who?
Les get something to eat – it's half time!

Knock Knock!
Who's there?
Luke!
Luke who?
Luke at me – I saved a penalty!

Knock Knock!
Who's there?
Stan!
Stan who?
Stan back – I'm going for goal!

Knock Knock!
Who's there?
Willy!
Willy who?
Willy score before the game ends?

EQUIPMENT QUIPS

Karen: I just got a football for my younger brother.
Minnie: That sounds like a good swap!

What runs around all day but lies still at night with its tongue hanging out?
A football boot!

What length must a football player's shorts be?
They must always be above two feet!

What did the right football boot say to the left football boot?
"Between us, we're going to have a ball!"

Which player in the World Cup has the biggest boots?
The one with the biggest feet!

Why do football pitches feel unloved?
Because they hate being treated like dirt!

What part of a football stadium is never the same each day?
The changing rooms!

When is a football not round?
When it's a long ball!

Why do footballers wear shorts?
Because if they didn't they'd be arrested!

What's black and white and wears a hat, coat and false moustache?
A football in disguise!

Which part of a pitch smells the best?
The scenter spot!

What should you do if you see a football flying through the air towards you?
Use your head!

What did the football say to the player?
"I get a kick out of you!"

How many footie supporters can you fit into an empty stadium?
One – after that it's not empty any more!

ENGLAND XI NAME GAME

Which England defender do the opposition find difficult to shake off?
Ledley Cling!

Which player is always worth two in the bush?
Rio Bird-in-hand!

Which defender causes problems by digging up the pitch?
Ashley Mole!

Which player prefers evening kick-offs?
Shaun Night-Phillips!

Which striker is a legendary footballer?
Alan Myth!

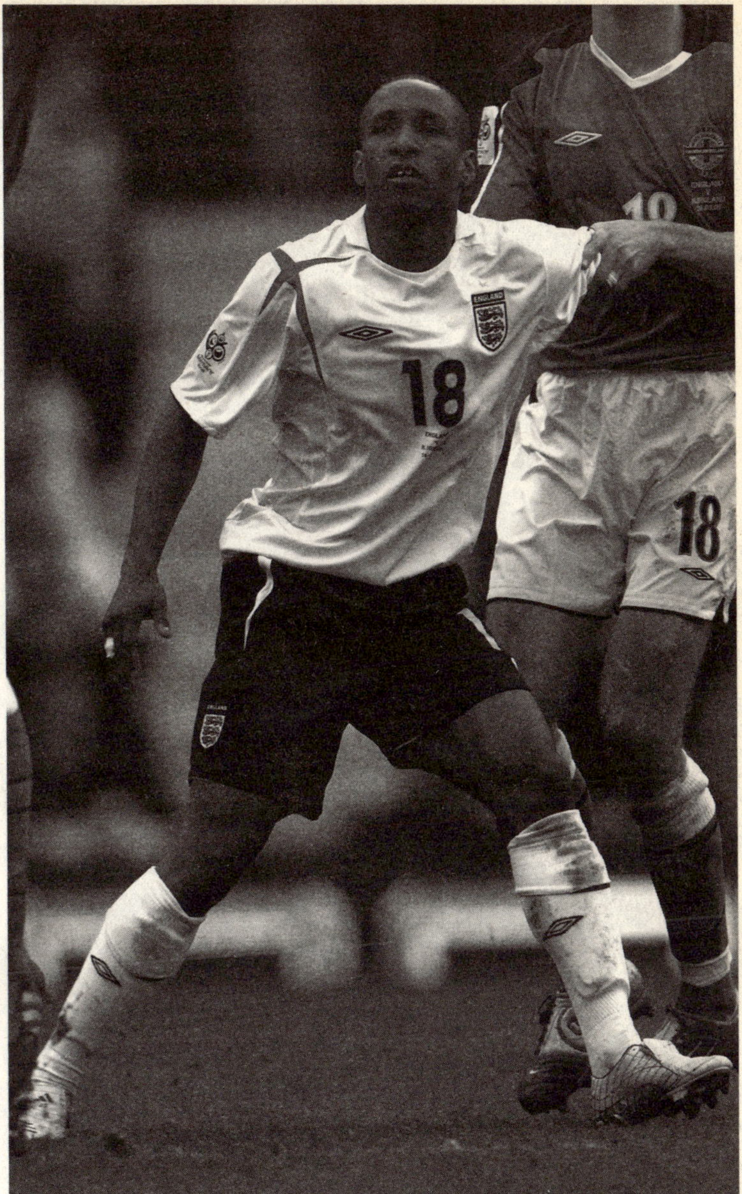
18
18

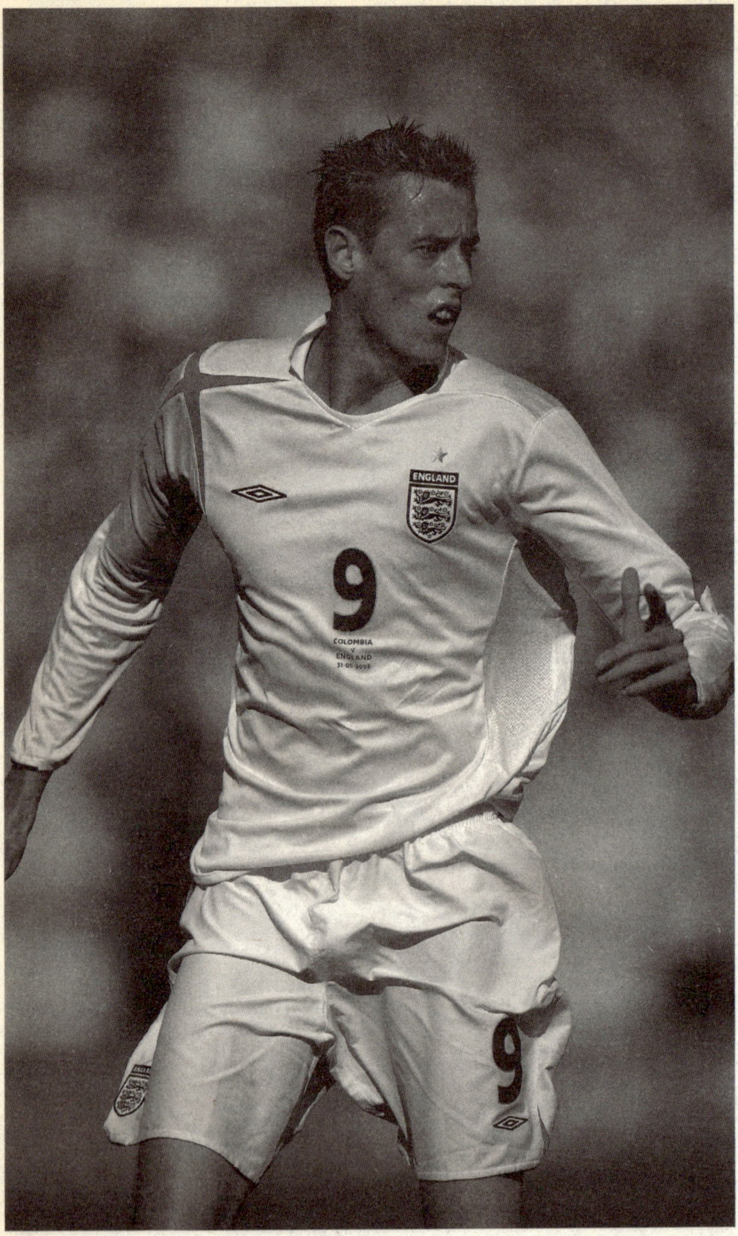
ENGLAND
9
COLOMBIA
v
ENGLAND
9

Which defender is always in a bad mood?
Wes Frown!

Which centre half is always in a good mood?
John Merry!

Which midfielder always looks like scoring?
Joe Goal!

EXTRA TIME TALES

Two old men, Gareth and Gordon, are queuing up to watch City play. When they get to the turnstile Gordon starts searching for his ticket. He hunts in his coat and trouser pockets but isn't having any luck. Then the turnstile operator notices something. **"You daft old fool,"** he says. **"There's a ticket sticking out of your mouth."**

Gordon pulls out the half-eaten ticket and is let through the turnstile.

"Oh dear," mutters Gareth. **"You really are getting forgetful in your old age."**

"Not really," chuckles Gordon. **"I was just chewing off last week's date!"**

Larry and Barry aren't able to watch England's match with Colombia live so Larry tapes it. The following day, the two footie fans sit down to watch the game.

"Tell you what, Barry," says Larry. **"I bet you £10 that England win."**

"I hope they do," replies Barry, "but I reckon Colombia will edge it. I'll accept the bet."

Larry and Barry cheer on the team as Michael Owen scores a hat trick to give England a 3-2 victory. When the final whistle goes, Barry hands his mate a £10 note.

"I can't take this," explains Larry, feeling guilty. "**I actually heard the score yesterday.**"

"Yeah, so did I," confesses his mate.

"Why on earth did you agree to the bet?" asks Larry, confused.

Barry answers, "**I just didn't think Colombia could lose a second time!**"

Rovers are leading 2-0 after 45 minutes and the manager is delighted. But by the time the final whistle blows, they've lost 4-2. The team are expecting the manager to shout at them. Instead he calmly asks if any of the players own a dog but no one does.

"That's no surprise," says the manager. "**None of you can hold onto a lead!**"

United are getting ready for the match when George the goalie arrives in a foul mood. "**Which one of you comedians hid all my clothes yesterday?**" he moans.

Nobody owns up so the manager asks where he found them.

"I didn't – and I looked for hours," Alex complains.

"So what did you go home in?" continues the manager.

Alex replies, "**The dark, of course!**"

Two aliens land on Earth and see a large group of people all walking down a road in the same direction. The aliens decide to follow and find themselves in a packed football stadium. They watch the players emerge from the tunnel and hear the referee blow his whistle. Forty-five minutes of uneventful footie follows and the teams troop off with the score at 0-0. The aliens stay in their seats during half-time, not sure what's happening. Then they see the players emerge from the tunnel and line up as the referee gets ready to start the second half.

"**No sense in watching it again,**" says one of the aliens. "**This is where we came in!**"

Owen, the Blues' goalie, is having a lousy game. In the first half he lets in three goals. "It can't get much worse," he thinks, trudging onto the pitch for the second half. But then it starts to rain – and the ground gets so muddy he keeps falling over when he races for the ball. When the final whistle goes, the Blues have lost 10-0.

Owen sits in the changing room, cold, wet and unhappy, when he suddenly starts sneezing. "**Oh great, now I've caught a cold,**" he whines.

"**That makes a change,**" says the skipper. "**It's the first thing you've caught all afternoon!**"

Wayne knocks on the door of his best friend's house. When his mate's mum answers, he asks, "**Can Steven come out to play?**".

"**No, he can't,**" answers Steven's mum. "**He's doing his homework.**"

Wayne continues, "**Well, can his football come out to play instead?**"

The Reds have lost 8-0 and the manager is telling the players

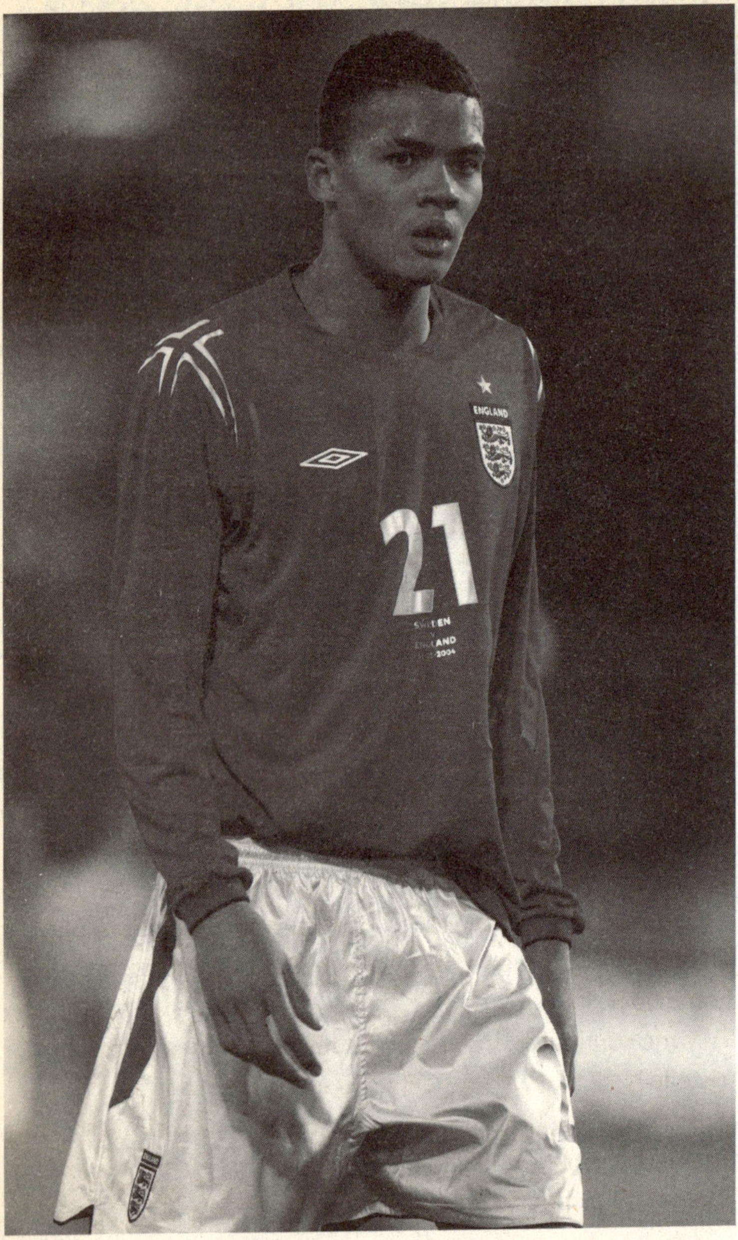
ENGLAND
21

exactly what he thinks of them. After 15 minutes of shouting, the skipper tries to defend the team's performance. **"It's just a minor blip, gaffer,"** he claims. **"After all, what's defeat?"**

"The things you should have been using to kick the ball," the manager replies!

Two fans, a young girl and an old man, are sitting next to each other waiting for the match to begin.

"I was a player when I was younger," says the old man.

"When was that?" asks the girl.

"It was almost 60 years ago," answers the man, **"but people still remember me. When I was in the car park earlier, lots of photographers swarmed round me and took my picture."**

"Really?" says the girl, doubtfully.

"Yes," replies the man. **"Just ask David Beckham – he was standing next to me at the time!"**

Paul has travelled to Germany for the World Cup but after arriving at the airport, he gets lost on the way to the game. He asks a policeman the best way to get to the Olympiastadion in Berlin. **"Practise!"** replies the policeman.

It's the day of the derby game between the Reds and the Blues. Guy, a Blues fan, is walking to the game, when he suddenly feels peckish. He spots a new café and goes inside to get some chips. It's very lively but as soon as Guy walks up to the counter the place falls silent. Guy suddenly realises all the customers and staff are wearing Reds shirts and the walls are covered with pictures of Reds players.

"We have a special game we play with Blues fans," says the café owner, slowly.

"What's that?" replies Guy, trying not to whimper.

"You get to roll this dice," explains the owner. "If you roll a one, two, three, four or five we all squirt ketchup over you so you can become a Red like us."

"But what if I get a six?" asks Guy, hopefully.

"Then you get to roll again!"

Rebecca arrives at a football match halfway through the second half. "Terrible traffic," she moans. **"What's the score?"**

"Nil-nil," replies the fan in the seat next to her.

"And what was the score at half time?" Rebecca asks.

IT'S OFFICIALS!

Ref: I'm sending you off.
Ruby: What for?
Ref: The rest of the match, of course!

Everyone knows there are referees in football and umpires in cricket, but what do you have in bowls?
Goldfish!
Who hangs out the team's kit after it's been washed?
The linesman!

Gemma: I'd like to be a referee. All they have to do is run after the ball.
Tessa: Yes, and after the match too, sometimes!

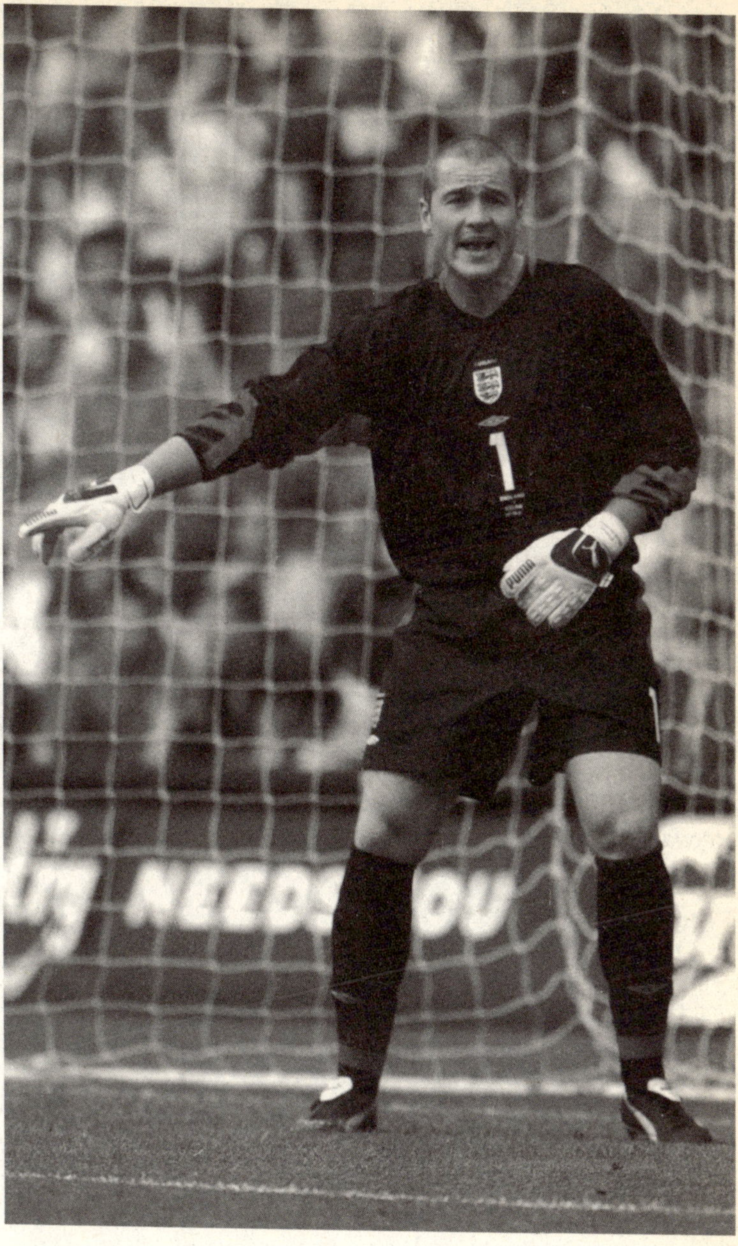
NEEDS

Fans were waiting for the game to begin when an announcement was made over the Tannoy. **"The referee is ill,"** began the voice. **"The match will be postponed unless anyone in the stands is a professional referee."**

One man stood up and went to the dug-out. **"I'm a referee,"** he said.

"Do you have any proof?" asked the club chairman.

"I don't have my licence here," explained the man, **"but you can ask my two mates I came with today."**

"Well, you can't be a real referee," blustered the chairman, **"not if you have two friends!"**

Why did the referee give the cockerel a yellow card?
For fowl behaviour!

Liam: I love watching football but I don't really understand all the rules.
Conrad: I guess you should become a referee then!

Why did the referee throw his watch in the air?
He wanted to see time fly!

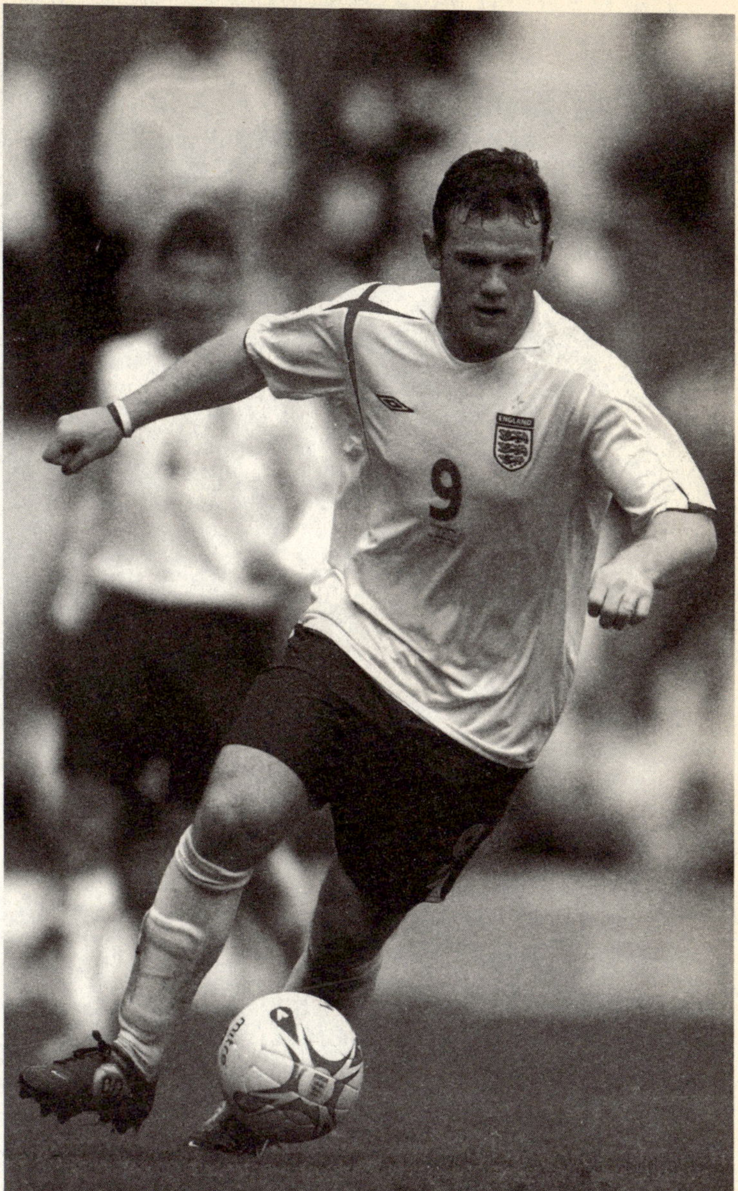
ENGLAND
9

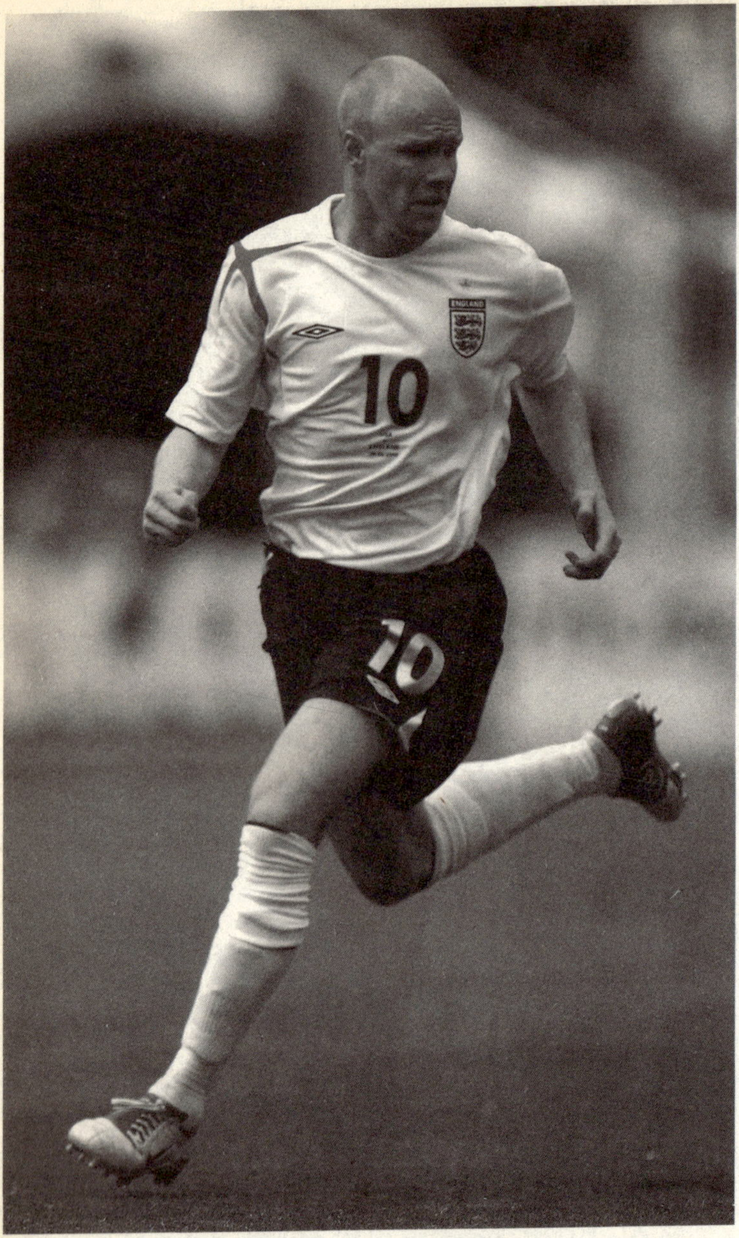
ENGLAND
10
10

SCHOOL SNIGGERS

Todd: Our school team is the best in the world – no one has ever scored against us!
Zach: Wow! How many games have you played?
Todd: The first one's next week...

Teacher: Why were you late for school today, boy?
Bob: I was dreaming about playing for England in the World Cup and the game went to penalties!

James: I've been asked to join the school football team. Mr Jones says he wants me to play very badly.
John: Just as well he doesn't want you to play well!

Teacher: How did the team get on in the match, Andy?
Andy: Like scrambled eggs, sir.
Teacher: Why were you like scrambled eggs?
Andy: Because we were well beaten!

Dan: Which position should I play this afternoon, sir?
Teacher: Hmm, I think you're going to be a centre back.
Stan: What about me, sir?
Teacher: Hmm, I think you're going to be a drawback.

Richard: That's another defeat for the school team!
Felix: Yeah, but for a minute I thought we had a chance...
Richard: When was that?
Felix: Before the game started!

Teacher: You stupid boy – you've got your boots on the wrong feet!
Hugh: But I don't have any other feet, sir!

Teacher: I want your kit to be in top condition for tomorrow's final. Make sure your socks don't have holes in them.
Lindsey: How will we get them on then, sir?

Teacher: I'll teach you to kick this football through the classroom window!
Derek: I wish you would, sir. I usually miss!

Teacher: Only two things are stopping you from becoming a famous footballer.
Terry: What two things?
Teacher: Your left foot and your right foot!

Headmaster: You've been sent to see me, Kevin, because you were caught fighting again with Keith. You must learn to give and take.
Kevin: I do, sir. I gave Keith a black eye and I took his football!

LAST GASP LAUGHS

Who delivers letters and parcels to football clubs?
The goalpost man!

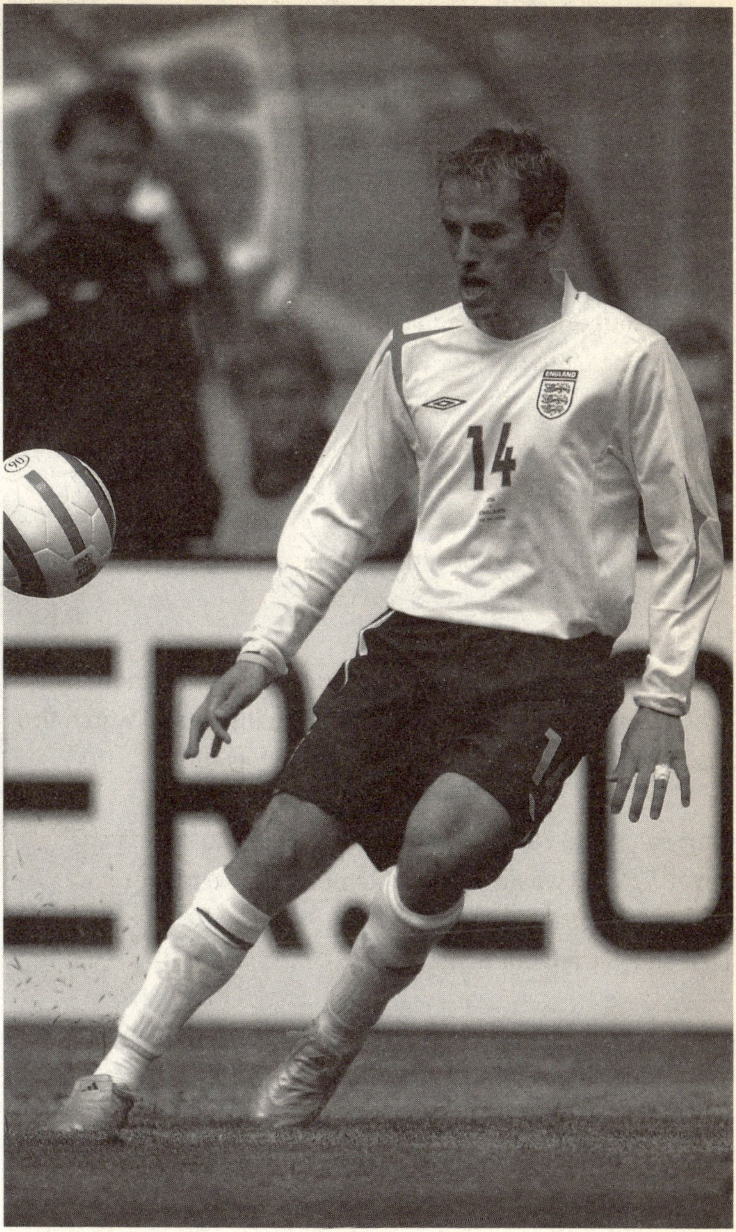
ENGLAND
14
ER.CO

How did the astronaut feel when his team won the World Cup?
Over the moon!

Why was the groundsman such a good singer?
Because he had a perfect pitch!

What's the difference between Prince Charles and a football seconds after it has been kicked over the touch-line?
The first is heir to the throne but the other is thrown in the air!

Why can't a car play football?
Because it's only got one boot!

Noah: Shall we go out and play football with your kid brother?
Nick: Shouldn't we use a real football?

The team manager spotted two boys climbing over the stadium wall. "Get back here," he shouted. "You'll stay and watch the match until the end like everyone else has to!"

Darren: I wish I'd brought our kitchen table to the match.
Ian: Why would you want to bring a table to a football game?
Darren: I've left our tickets on it!

Why did the football team hire a baby ghost to be its mascot?
It wanted a little team spirit!

What do you do when you're too hot at a football match?
Sit next to a fan!

Park keeper: Why are you boys playing football on the climbing frame?
Rex: Because the sign said no ball games on the grass!

Sally: Excuse me, librarian. Do you have Couldn't Hit A Barn Door by Miss D. Goal?
Librarian: No, but we do have a copy of Too Many Headers by I C Starrs!

Emma: Excuse me, sir. I've come to watch the match with my dad but we've become separated in the crowd. Can you help me find him?
Policeman: Of course, young lady. What's he like?
Emma: Er, football, curry and telly!

Tournament Tales

The World Cup isn't just packed with great goals and nail-biting matches – it's also the place for some brilliantly bizarre behaviour!

URUGUAY '30

HAVING A BALL
The first ever World Cup final was a six-goal thriller between two South American teams – Uruguay and Argentina. But even before the match kicked off, the two teams were battling it out – over which football to use! Each team brought a ball and wanted to play with it in the final. Finally it was agreed that the Argentinean ball would be used in the first half and Uruguay's ball in the second half!

And it's no wonder the teams argued – each side played their best football when using their own ball. At half-time, Argentina were leading 2-1 but then Uruguay's ball was introduced. The host nation scored three times in the second half and won the match 4-2!

FRANCE '38

SHORTS STORY
Spectators at the semi-final between Italy and Brazil in 1938 saw a bit more than they were expecting. Italy took the lead early in the second half thanks to a goal from Gino Colaussi. Minutes later, life looked even bleaker for the Brazilians when Italy were awarded a penalty. Captain Giuseppe Meazza was about to put

the ball on the spot – just as the string on his shorts broke and they fell down!

The crowd's laughter echoed around the stadium. But Meazza carefully pulled his shorts up and put the ball down. Still clutching his kit, Italy's captain took his run-up and fired the ball into the net past Brazil's goalie, Walter. Perhaps the keeper was tired from playing in a quarter-final replay two days before – or maybe he was too shocked by what he'd seen. Either way, Italy won the game and then the final, proving they were no flash in the pan!

BRAZIL '50

GIVEN THE BOOT?
Many countries withdrew from the 1950 tournament leaving just 13 teams to contest the finals. Argentina didn't take part because of an argument with the Brazilian Federation. Portugal were offered a place but turned it down once they'd discovered their first round matches would take place 3,200km apart. Austria, Syria, Turkey, Belgium, Scotland, France, Ecuador, Peru, Burma and Philippines all said thanks but no thanks too! Perhaps the strangest reason for withdrawing came from India. The team wanted to play in bare feet but FIFA wouldn't allow it, so they decided not to compete!

SWEDEN '58

BY GUM!
Wales reached the quarter-finals in 1958, losing to the eventual champions Brazil by a single goal. Much of the team's success

was down to their goalkeeper Jack Kelsey, who made some dramatic saves during the tournament. A former steelworker, Arsenal keeper Kelsey was famous for having hands the size of dinner plates! He also had a secret weapon to help him hang onto the ball – chewing gum! Before each match he would rub it into his hands. So it was probably best not to head the ball straight after Kelsey had been holding it!

ENGLAND '66

IN A PICKLE...

England famously won the World Cup in 1966 but the players might not have got their hands on the trophy if it hadn't been for a mongrel called Pickles. On 20th March the trophy was stolen from an exhibition in London. Holders Brazil were furious and claimed that such a theft would never happen in their country. The police were hunting for a suspect with black hair and a scar on his face but seemed baffled. It turns out the one lead they should have been following was the one connected to Pickles the dog! The mongrel was walking with his owner in south London a week after the theft and found the trophy hidden under a bush. For his dogged detection work, Pickles was invited to England's victory party at the end of the tournament!

MEXICO '70

STRIP – OFF!

Most of the fans packed in Mexico City's Azteca Stadium to watch the 1970 final were rooting for Brazil to win and they weren't disappointed. Pelé and Jairzinho were amongst the

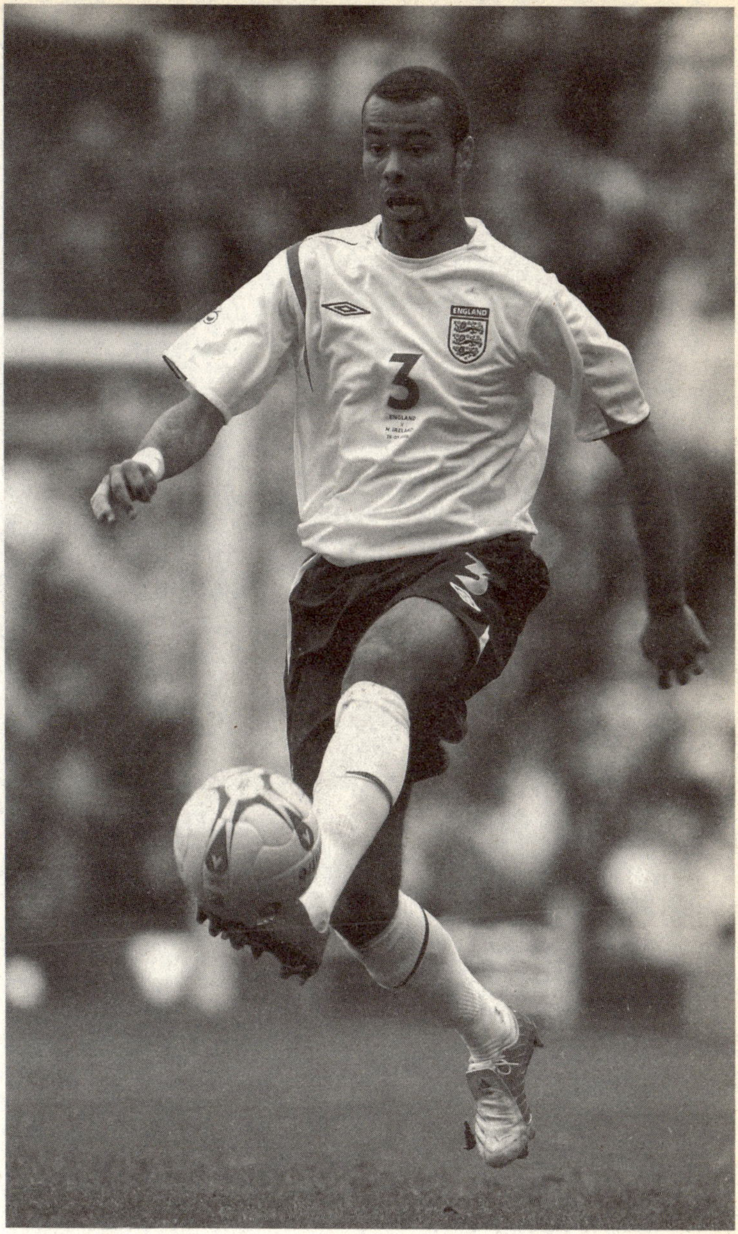
ENGLAND
3

72

scorers as the South Americans beat Italy 4-1. Magnificent striker Tostão later claimed that he didn't see the final goal because he was crying with joy for the last 15 minutes. But telly watchers around the world certainly saw more of Tostão than usual! At the final whistle hordes of fans swept onto the pitch eager to claim a souvenir – and Tostão was soon stripped down to his blue underpants. It's a good job they weren't in Brazil's team colours too!

WEST GERMANY '74

NET RESULT

Zaire's record at the '74 finals wasn't too impressive. They played three and lost three, letting in 14 goals and scoring none. The worst result came against Yugoslavia. Zaire were losing 0-3 and coach Blagoje Vidinic decided that the keeper, Kazadi Muamba, was to blame. Muamba was hauled off and substitute Dimbi Tubilandu took his place between the posts. It proved to be a great decision – for Yugoslavia! They scored another six goals, winning the game 9-0. Coach Vidinic might have had mixed emotions at the result – he was Yugoslavian and used to play for the national team. His position? Goalkeeper, of course!

SPAIN '82

WHISTLE-STOP APPEARANCE

The match between France and Kuwait had a weird pitch invasion – by a prince! France were leading 3-1 when they thought they had added a fourth. But the Kuwaiti players claimed they had heard a whistle and stopped playing. They refused to continue the game and the president of the Kuwaiti Federation, Prince Fahid Al-Ahmad Al-Sabah, even ended up on the pitch to talk to the referee and the players. Play finally resumed with ref Miroslav Stupar bizarrely disallowing the goal and awarding a drop ball! France did score again later in the game and this time the goal was allowed. FIFA later fined Kuwait for the chaos they caused on the pitch.

ITALY '90

ROLLS WITH IT
Hugging team-mates... performing a series of acrobatic back flips... most goal scorers can't hide their feelings when they find the back of the net. But in the 1990 tournament, the United Arab Emirates players had a very good reason to celebrate. The government promised that anyone who scored a goal would be given a Rolls Royce! So even though the team lost all of their first round matches and conceded 11 goals, Khalid Mubarak and Ali Thani Juma'a had a lot to be happy about – they each scored a goal and picked up a Roller!

FRANCE '98

PERFECT MATCH
In the first round of France '98, Norway needed to beat Brazil to guarantee a spot in the last 16. With such a vital game, you wouldn't have thought there would be much love lost between the two sets of fans... but you'd be wrong. Before the match started Norwegian Oivind Ekeland and Brazilian Rosangela de

Souza walked onto the pitch and got married in front of 60,000 spectators! The bride wore a white dress and tiara. The groom wore a Brazil number nine jersey with Ronaldo written across the back and a black top hat. And Oivind was no doubt even happier when Norway beat Brazil 2-1. But the story has a happy ending as the result meant both Norway and Brazil qualified for the next round!

JAPAN AND SOUTH KOREA '02

AUSSIE RULES!

Australia narrowly missed out on a place in the 2002 finals, losing a play-off against Uruguay, who did go through. But whilst attempting to qualify they did set an amazing record – the most goals scored in an international match. On 11th April 2001 Australia played American Samoa... and won 31-0! The first goal wasn't scored until the eighth minute but then the onslaught began. Archie Thompson notched up another record, finding the back of the net 13 times – that's four hat tricks plus one for luck. At the time the match was played, American Samoa were ranked 203rd in the world. Their qualifying results certainly back this up – played four, lost four, no goals scored and 57 conceded!

BOG OFF, BYRON

Byron Moreno probably won't be visiting Italy for his holidays. The Ecuadorean referee was in charge of the second round game between Italy and South Korea. The home side won 2-1, scoring a golden goal in extra time. But this came after Moreno disallowed a goal by Italy, turned down their appeal for a penalty

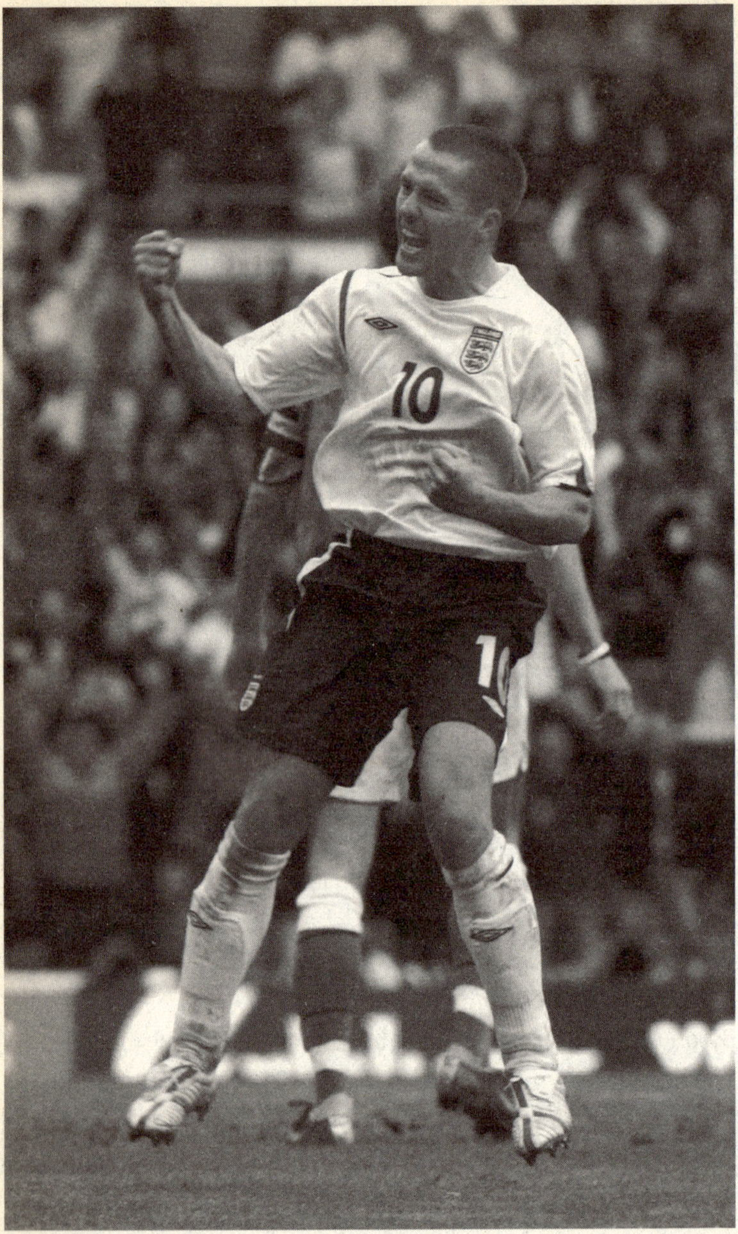
10

and sent off Francesco Totti for diving!

Unsurprisingly, the Italian fans were somewhat miffed. So when four new public loos were built in the resort of Santa Teresa Riva in Sicily two months later, it was decided to name them after the unpopular referee. Mayor Nino Bartolotta agreed that Moreno nameplates could be attached to the block of bogs. One city official claimed it was a great opportunity for locals and tourists "to remember Moreno's performance at the World Cup"!

England Enigmas

How much do you know about England's World Cup stars past and present? The next three pages should give you a clue!

ENGLAND EXPECTS...
Are you an England ace? Find out with these ten questions about the team's World Cup exploits.

TOUGH TO TACKLE...
1. How many World Cup finals have England played in, between 1930 and 2002?

2. In 1950, England won their first ever World Cup finals match 2-0. Who were their opponents?
   a) Brazil
   b) Chile
   c) Spain
   d) USA

3. "England will win the World Cup in 1966," predicted the team's new manager in 1963. Who was it?
   a) Ron Greenwood
   b) Alf Ramsey
   c) Don Revie
   d) Walter Winterbottom

4. True or false?
   England drew every single one of their qualification games for Mexico '70 – and just squeezed through on goal difference.

5. Which of these famous players only appeared in one World Cup finals game?
    a) Terry Butcher
    b) Steve Coppell
    c) Kevin Keegan
    d) Graeme Le Saux

6. England scored their fastest goal in a World Cup finals game at Spain '82. France found themselves 1-0 down after just 27 seconds – but who found the back of the net?
    a) Trevor Brooking
    b) Glenn Hoddle
    c) Bryan Robson
    d) Ray Wilkins

7. At Spain '82, England didn't lose any of their five games but still didn't reach the semi-finals. True or false?

8. England's qualifying group for the 2002 finals included Germany. Playing at home England lost 0-1 but the team recorded a famous victory in Germany. What was the score?
    a) Germany 0 England 3
    b) Germany 1 England 4
    c) Germany 1 England 5
    d) Germany 2 England 6

9. Who was England's top scorer at Japan and South Korea '02?
    a) David Beckham
    b) Rio Ferdinand

c) Emile Heskey
d) Michael Owen

TOUGH TO TACKLE...

10. Which team have England played the most times at World Cup finals tournaments?

Squad Shake-Up

Here are some of England's stars hoping to shine in the 2006 World Cup. Can you unscramble the letters to reveal their names?

1. EYE ON NORWAY = _ _ _ _ _ _ _ _ _ _ _

2. FINER ANDRIOD = _ _ _ _ _ _ _ _ _ _ _

3. CEASE HOLLY = _ _ _ _ _ _ _ _ _ _

4. COMPELS BALL = _ _ _ _ _ _ _ _ _ _

5. DRAGSTER NERVE = _ _ _ _ _ _ _ _ _ _ _ _ _

6. FARMLAND PARK = _ _ _ _ _ _ _ _ _ _ _ _

7. NO AVERAGE SHREW = _ _ _ _ _ _ _ _ _ _ _ _ _

8. SAME NINJA JEER = _ _ _ _ _ _ _ _ _ _ _ _ _

9. POLAR BUNIONS = _ _ _ _ _ _ _ _ _ _ _

10. WHOLE CINEMA = _ _ _ _ _ _ _ _ _ _ _

'66 Heroes

The eleven England stars who played in the 1966 World Cup final are hidden in the grid below. Their names run horizontally, vertically and diagonally and can be forwards or backwards. How quickly can you find them?

- BALL
- BANKS
- B CHARLTON
- J CHARLTON
- COHEN
- HUNT
- HURST
- MOORE
- PETERS
- STILES
- WILSON

```
H N F L H W S S C T
B S O U L E U R O N
C A R T L A J E H U
Z S N I L A B T E H
T P T K M R Z E N D
C S Q U S A A P U T
W I L S O N B H V B
J I V E R O O M C U
N O T L R A H C B J
F V M J V G X N N W
```

Forward Thinking

The clues below will help you uncover the identity of a famous forward. How many do you need before you can guess his identity?

1. This talented player was born on 30th November 1960.

2. He appeared in two World Cup finals in 1986 and 1990 and played in 12 games.

3. He might not have won a World Cup final but he did get his hands on the Spanish Cup, the European Cup Winners' Cup and The FA Cup.

4. He played for Leicester City, Everton, Barcelona, Tottenham Hotspur and Grampus Eight.

5. He received 80 caps for England and scored a hugely impressive 48 goals.

6. He always obeyed the rules of the game – during his whole playing career, he was never shown a red or yellow card.

7. He won the Golden Boot at the 1986 World Cup, scoring six goals.

8. He now appears on telly hosting Match of the Day – and eating a lot of crisps!

He Shoots....

Can you match the England goal-scorers with the right World Cup? Each player found the back of the net at one tournament, although some played but didn't score at other World Cup finals.

THE TOURNAMENTS	THE PLAYERS
Brazil '50	Peter Beardsley
Switzerland '54	Jimmy Greaves
Sweden '58	Emile Heskey
Chile '62	Roger Hunt
England '66	Derek Kevan
Mexico '70	Nat Lofthouse
Spain '82	Wilf Mannion
Mexico '86	Alan Mullery
Italy '90	David Platt
France '98	Bryan Robson
Japan and South Korea '02	Alan Shearer

Memorable Mug

This could be one of the greatest footballers in the world – because it's three current England stars squeezed into one. Which three players can you identify in this picture? There's one defender, one midfielder and one striker to be found.

Summer of '66

Five questions to test your knowledge of the victorious '66 team

1. England played six games at the 1966 World Cup and won five of them. Which team did they fail to beat?
   a) Argentina
   b) France
   c) Mexico
   d) Uruguay

2. Who scored England's first goal at the tournament?
   a) Bobby Charlton
   b) Jimmy Greaves
   c) Bobby Moore
   d) Martin Peters

3. Hat trick hero Geoff Hurst replaced the injured Jimmy Greaves in the team. Hurst's first game at the tournament was the final itself – true or false?

TOUGH TO TACKLE...
4. How many England players appeared in all six of the team's matches?

5. During the tournament, Jack Charlton was randomly selected four times to give a urine sample for a drugs test. Because he'd been picked so many times, the testers presented him with a baby's potty! True or false?

New King Cole

"And Ledley King passes to Ashley Cole..."

But can you turn King into Cole using the clues below. Change one letter each time to make a new word.

KING

1. _ _ _ _   Seen on birds, bats and aeroplanes!

2. _ _ _ _   Alcoholic drink made from grapes...

3. _ _ _ _   ...which grow on this plant

4. _ _ _ _   Disgusting and shameful

5. _ _ _ _   Small mouse-like rodent

COLE

Captain Marvels

The nine players listed below have all captained England in a World Cup finals match. Your task is to fit them all into the grid – Good luck!

- ❏ BECKHAM
- ❏ BUTCHER
- ❏ HAYNES
- ❏ MILLS
- ❏ MOORE
- ❏ ROBSON
- ❏ SHEARER
- ❏ SHILTON
- ❏ WRIGHT

```
Y M A H K C E B N R
R I E W N W B O O O
X E R R R G T K I B
Q X H I O L I R D S
O F G C I O I E S O
L H E H T W M R Y N
T L S Z A U V A Z K
H A Y N E S B E D U
O O S L L I M H G V
G A I P I Z F S T V
```

Missing Men

This team photo was taken at England's qualifying game against Azerbaijan in March 2005. But four of the players have disappeared! Can you guess who is missing from the starting line-up?

QUICK CLUE

Read this backwards to get an extra clue
slived der neeb lla evah yehT

Charltons Athletic

The Charlton brothers, Bobby and Jack, both helped England win the World Cup. Below are ten facts about the terrific twosome. Five of them relate to Bobby and five are about Jack – can you sort out which is which?

1. _____ is the older of the two brothers

2. _____ worked in a coal mine and applied to join the police before becoming a footballer

3. _____ played for Manchester United from 1956 to 1973

4. _____ was voted European Footballer of the Year in 1966

5. _____ was awarded the Footballer of the Year award in 1967 – and his long acceptance speech was given a standing ovation

6. _____ scored a record 49 goals for England

7. _____ played for England 106 times – only Bobby Moore and Peter Shilton have received more caps

8. _____ notched up a record 629 appearances for Leeds

9. _____ became Ireland's manager in 1986 and took the team to the World Cup in 1990 and 1994

10. _____ received a knighthood in 1994

Get The Balls Rolling

There are a few too many balls here, as we've added an extra five! Looking at the position of the players, can you work out which is the real ball?

Classic Confusion

Here are the names of 10 famous England players but the letters have all been mixed-up. Can you solve the anagrams? The dates tell you which World Cups they played in to give you a clue.

1. **TALENT SWAYS THEM** (1950, 1954)
   = _ _ _ _ _ _ _ _ _ _ _ _ _ _

2. **NOBLY BOTCH BAR** (1962, 1966, 1970)
   = _ _ _ _ _ _ _ _ _ _ _ _ _

3. **BE BROOM BOY** (1962, 1966, 1970)
   = _ _ _ _ _ _ _ _ _ _

4. **RAFT CONS RIVER** (1982)
   = _ _ _ _ _ _ _ _ _ _ _ _ _ _

5. **SHELTER POINT** (1982, 1986, 1990)
   = _ _ _ _ _ _ _ _ _ _ _ _

6. **REAL KEY RING** (1986, 1990)
   = _ _ _ _ _ _ _ _ _ _ _

7. **OGLE CUPS AGAIN** (1990)
   = _ _ _ _   _ _ _ _ _ _ _ _ _

8. **HEAR ARSENAL** (1998)
   = _ _ _ _   _ _ _ _ _ _ _

9. **INVADES A DAM** (1998, 2002)
   = _ _ _ _ _   _ _ _ _ _ _

10. **LOCAL PUSHES** (1998, 2002)
    = _ _ _ _   _ _ _ _ _ _ _

Nearly in '90

Apart from 1966, England's best performance at a World Cup tournament was at Italy '90. Time to find out how much you know about the team's performance...

TOUGH TO TACKLE...

1. England's qualifying group for the finals contained Albania, Poland and Sweden. How many goals did England concede over the six matches?

2. Who was England's manager at Italy '90?
   a) Ron Greenwood
   b) Glenn Hoddle
   c) Bobby Robson
   d) Graham Taylor

3. Who was England's top scorer at the tournament?
   a) John Barnes
   b) Peter Beardsley
   c) Gary Lineker
   d) David Platt

4. After being shown a yellow card in the semi-final, Stuart Pearce burst into tears on the pitch, realising that he couldn't play in the final if England qualified.
   True or false?

5. Which of these awards did England receive at Italy '90?
   a) Bronze third place medals
   b) FIFA Fair Play Award
   c) FIFA Award for the Most Entertaining team
   d) The Golden Net award for the team scoring the most goals at a tournament

Star Search

Hidden in the grid below are all the England players who played in the 2002 World Cup finals. Names can be found horizontally, vertically, diagonally and forwards and backwards.

```
G W J U R D A V I D S E A M A N
D N A I D R E F O I R P A T R
S O L C A M P B E L L K T H T E
I K W R L E M I L E H E S K E Y
O P H E C U B B B V H G T C T D
M A H G N I R E H S Y D D E T N
I U S B I H U T E F N I E B U O
C L L E S S A V S U I R A D B R
H S L L R R C R A W N B Q I Y E
A C I O O S B C G U A E T V K I
E H M C V T Y A W R H N Y A C K
L O Y E E I I G F A E Y U D I M
O L N O R W F B L C P A C S N E
W E N J T J L H E H S W V H R G
E S A R O B B I E F O W L E R N
N C D T S L E L O C Y E L H S A
```

DAVID BECKHAM KIERON DYER MICHAEL OWEN
WAYNE BRIDGE RIO FERDINAND PAUL SCHOLES
NICKY BUTT ROBBIE FOWLER DAVID SEAMAN
SOL CAMPBELL OWEN HARGREAVES TEDDY SHERINGHAM
ASHLEY COLE EMILE HESKEY TREVOR SINCLAIR
JOE COLE DANNY MILLS DARIUS VASSELL

Perfect Defender

Three current England players have kindly donated parts of their bodies to create the Perfect Defender below. You need to identify two defenders and one midfielder.

Can we have our ball back?

Joe Cole is seen here scoring against Northern Ireland in a World Cup qualifying match. Can you mark an X in the grid square you think the ball should be in?

Keeper Conundrum

England have had some great keepers over the years. Gordon Banks was first choice for the '66 and '70 tournaments, Peter Shilton was between the posts in 1982, 1986 and 1990 and David Seaman took over for France '98 and Japan and South Korea '02. Can you connect each goalie to three facts from the list below?

THE KEEPERS
A. GORDON BANKS   B. PETER SHLTON   C. DAVID SEAMAN

1. .... saved a shot from Pelé at one finals that was nicknamed 'Save of the Century'!

2. .... played in 17 World Cup finals matches

3. .... kept a clean sheet against Tunisia in his first World Cup finals game and played his last finals game against Brazil

4. .... played for England a record 125 times

5. .... played his first and last games for England against Scotland

6. .... is Stoke City's most-capped player

7. .... played for a number of League clubs, including Peterborough, Birmingham City and Queens Park Rangers

8. .... was player/manager of Plymouth Argyle for three years

9. .... won The FA Cup and the League Cup in the same season

Player Puzzle

How many clues do you need before you can identify this famous England player?

1. He was born on 8th December 1941 in Ashton-under-Lyne

3. He played for West Ham United, Stoke City and West Bromwich Albion

2. Between 1959 and 1972 he played 410 League games for West Ham United

6. He managed Chelsea between 1979 and 1981

4. His six World Cup finals appearances were at England '66 and Mexico '70

5. He played for England 49 times and scored 24 goals

6. As well as helping England win the World Cup, he also picked up The FA Cup and the European Cup Winners' Cup

7. He is the only player to have scored a hat trick in a World Cup final

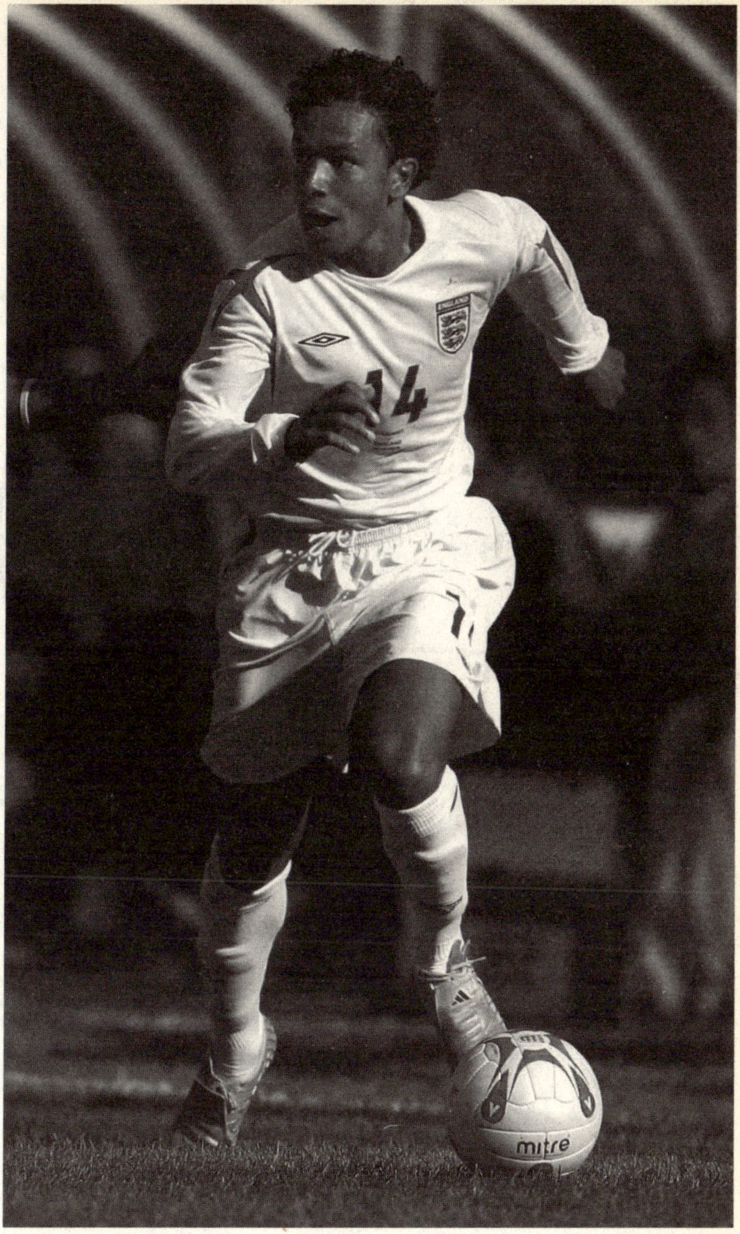
ENGLAND
14
mitre

Shoot on site

Which route to goal is successful for Darren Bent?

Qualification Quiz

These questions are all about England's route to Germany '06. Can you score five out of five?

TOUGH TO TACKLE...

1. Which midfielder scored England's first goal of the 2006 qualifying campaign?

2. And which date did that first match take place on?
   a) 1st March 2004
   b) 2nd May 2004
   c) 3rd July 2004
   d) 4th September 2004

3. Which of these teams was not in England's 2006 World Cup qualifying group?
   a) Albania
   b) Austria
   c) Poland
   d) Wales

4. England beat Northern Ireland 4-0 in a qualifier on 26th March 2005. Which of these players didn't get on the score-sheet?
   a) Joe Cole
   b) Frank Lampard
   c) Michael Owen
   d) Wayne Rooney

5. As Wembley Stadium wasn't available, England played all their home qualifying games at Manchester United's ground, Old Trafford. True or false?

Squad Squares

Can you fit all the England footballers in the grid below, ignoring the spaces between first names and surnames? All these players featured in England's World Cup qualifier against Azerbaijan on 30th March 2005.

```
D P R X E D D M N N
N N H H E L A T O E
L M A F V H O G S V
R A O N K X N C N I
E E M C I I Y B I L
Y H E P K D F J B L
D B C N A V R W O E
G E R R A R D E R U
Y R R E T X D N F T
T O W E N U X P F M
```

- ❏ BECKHAM
- ❏ COLE
- ❏ DEFOE
- ❏ DYER
- ❏ FERDINAND
- ❏ GERRARD
- ❏ KING
- ❏ LAMPARD
- ❏ NEVILLE
- ❏ OWEN
- ❏ ROBINSON
- ❏ ROONEY
- ❏ TERRY

Spot the difference

These are two pictures of the England team before a World Cup qualifier. They might look the same but they're not. There are five differences between the two – and it's your job to find them!

Three... Two... One...

Here are the names of 12 England stars who will be hoping to appear in Germany. Four of them played in their first World Cup finals in France in 1998 and another four had their first taste at Japan and South Korea in 2002. The final four haven't played in a World Cup finals match... yet! Can you put the players in the right places?

1. World Cup finals debut at France '98

2. World Cup finals debut at Japan and South Korea '02

3. Haven't yet appeared in a World Cup finals game

DAVID BECKHAM	RIO FERDINAND	GARY NEVILLE
SOL CAMPBELL	STEVEN GERRARD	MICHAEL OWEN
ASHLEY COLE	OWEN HARGREAVES	PAUL ROBINSON
JOE COLE	FRANK LAMPARD	JOHN TERRY

World Cup Challenges - Second Half

Time to bamboozle your brain with quizzes on all the World Cups from Argentina 1978 to this year's tournament in Germany

Argentina '78 Quick Quiz

WINNERS ARGENTINA

1. For the first time ever, over 100 countries attempted to qualify for the World Cup finals, hoping to win a place in Argentina. True or false?

2. The opening match between Poland and West Germany ended without a goal. Before 1978, when was the last time someone had scored in the opening game of a World Cup finals?
    a) 1974
    b) 1970
    c) 1966
    d) 1962

3. In the first round game between Brazil and Sweden why was a goal by Zico disallowed?
    a) Zico pushed the ball into the net with his hands
    b) The referee had been knocked unconscious by the Swedish goalie

c) The referee blew the whistle for full time just before the ball crossed the line
   d) Zico was a Brazilian fan who had crept onto the pitch and played for 10 minutes before anyone noticed

4. Why was Holland's Dick Nanninga shown the red card after playing for just eight minutes against West Germany in a second round match?
   a) Making rude gestures to the German fans
   b) Laughing at the referee
   c) Removing his shirt after scoring a goal
   d) Grabbing the linesman's flag after being ruled offside

TOUGH TO TACKLE...

5. In their last second round game, Argentina needed to beat Peru by better than 4-1 to reach the final. Sounds tough? Luckily for them, Peru failed to find the net, but how many goals did Argentina score?

Spain '82 Quick Quiz

WINNERS ITALY

1. More teams took part in the 1982 finals than ever before. How many countries lined up in Spain?
   a) 16
   b) 20
   c) 24
   d) 30

TOUGH TO TACKLE...

2. Here are France's three match results from group one:

   England 3   France 1
   France 4   Kuwait 1
   France 1   Czechoslovakia 1

   How many points did they pick up from those three games?

3. Northern Ireland's first round group included the host nation Spain, Yugoslavia and Honduras. Keeper Pat Jennings let in an unlucky 13 goals as Northern Ireland crashed to defeat in all three games. True or false?

4. El Salvador suffered a record World Cup finals defeat when they were beaten 10-1 in the first round. Who were their opponents?
   a) Algeria
   b) Cameroon
   c) Czechoslovakia
   d) Hungary

5. The first World Cup game to be decided by a penalty shoot-out took place in 1982. Which teams were involved?
   a) Brazil and Argentina
   b) France and Austria
   c) Italy and Poland
   d) West Germany and France

Record Breakers

Amazing football is guaranteed at Germany 2006 – and there might even be some record breakers. Match these 10 football feats with the current record holders.

> **WARNING! There are ten records and ten names. But two players share one record and one player holds two records!**

WORLD CUP FINALS RECORDS

A Youngest player

B Oldest player

C Youngest scorer

D Oldest scorer

E Most appearances in finals

F Fastest goal

G Fastest red card

H Most goals scored in one tournament

I Most goals scored from all tournaments

J Most clean sheets

HALL OF FAME

Antonio Carbajal (Mexico)

Just Fontaine (France)

Lothar Matthäus (West Germany/Germany)

Roger Milla (Cameroon)

Gerd Müller (West Germany)

Pelé (Brazil)

Peter Shilton (England)

Hakan Sukur (Turkey)

Sergio Batista (Uruguay)

Norman Whiteside (Northern Ireland)

Mexico '86 Quick Quiz

WINNERS ARGENTINA

1. Mexico became the first country to hold the finals twice. Which country had been chosen as the original host but withdrew because of the expense of staging the tournament?
   a) Colombia
   b) Ecuador
   c) Peru
   d) Venezuela

2. One team were competing in Mexico in their second World Cup finals. Their only other appearance had been in 1970... in Mexico! Which team was it?
   a) Algeria
   b) Canada
   c) Iraq
   d) Morocco

3. The first round group featuring England, Poland, Portugal and Morocco was nicknamed the 'Group of the Sleeping' by local Mexicans. This was because the matches were played in incredibly hot and humid conditions causing several players to pass out.
   True or false?

TOUGH TO TACKLE...

4. The format of the finals was changed again in 1986, with 52 matches being played. After the first 36 matches had taken place over a hectic two weeks, how many of the 24 teams taking part were still left in the competition?

5. How many of the quarter-finals ended in penalty shoot-outs?

Italy '90 Quick Quiz

WINNERS WEST GERMANY

1. 1990 saw a new record for bookings in a World Cup tournament. How many yellow and red cards were dished out?
   a) 112 yellows and 10 reds
   b) 137 yellows and 12 reds
   c) 151 yellows and 14 reds
   d) 164 yellows and 16 reds

2. Which of these statements is not correct?
   a) 1990 was the first time the Republic of Ireland reached the World Cup finals
   b) In a high-scoring first round game, the Republic thrashed Egypt 7-2
   c) David O'Leary only played in one game, coming on as a substitute against Romania. He still helped take Ireland through to the quarter-finals by scoring the winner in a penalty shoot-out
   d) Ireland's Mick McCarthy committed more fouls than any other player at the 1990 World Cup

TOUGH TO TACKLE...

3. Italy met Argentina in the semi-finals and the two sides were certainly used to playing each other. Before 1990, which was the most recent World Cup tournament not to feature a game between these two sides?

4. West Germany met Argentina in the final – just as they had in the previous tournament in 1986. This was the first time the same two countries had contested two World Cup finals in a row – true or false?

5. Argentina's Gustavo Dezotti became the first person to be sent off in a World Cup final at Italy '90. True or false?

USA '94 Quick Quiz

WINNERS BRAZIL

1. How many UK teams took part in the World Cup in USA?
   a) 0
   b) 1
   c) 2
   d) 3

2. In the first round game between Russia and Cameroon Roger Milla became the oldest player to score a World Cup goal. Another finals record was broken in the same game – what was it?
   a) Most goals scored by one player in a game
   b) Smallest audience for a finals game
   c) Most players sent off in one game
   d) Longest amount of extra time played

TOUGH TO TACKLE...

3. Bulgaria reached the semi-finals – a great achievement for a team which had never won a World Cup finals game before, having appeared in five previous tournaments. How many finals games did Bulgaria play before they notched up their first famous victory?

4. Mexico were one of the teams knocked out by the improved Bulgarians. It was amazing anyone got the ball past the Mexican keeper, Jorges Campos... and weren't distracted by his hideous shirt instead! Campos was very proud of his colourful kit because famous designer Calvin Klein had created it for him – true or false?

5. This was the first World Cup final to be settled by a penalty shoot-out. True or false?

All Change

These two pictures from England's World Cup qualifying match againgst Azerbijan might look the same but there are five differences between the two. How quickly can you find them?

Star Striker

How quickly can you identify the famous footballer from the clues below?

1. He was born on 23rd October 1940

2. He made his League debut for Santos in 1956 when he was aged just 15

3. He made his World Cup debut in 1958 against the former USSR

4. His first World Cup goal was against Wales and he scored a hat trick against France

5. In 1958 he became the youngest ever member of a World Cup winning team

6. He is the only player to have won three World Cups – in 1958, 1962 and 1970

7. He scored 77 goals for Brazil in 92 appearances

8. He was born Edson Arantes do Nascimento but is better known by a single four letter name

France '98 Quick Quiz

WINNERS FRANCE

1. FIFA adopted a new system in 1998, seeding one team in each of the first round groups. They did a good Mystic Meg act as seven of the eight teams finished top of their groups. Which one didn't?
   a) Brazil
   b) Italy
   c) Romania
   d) Spain

2. Japan made their debut finals appearance in 1998 – but probably wished they hadn't. They were the only team to lose all their first round games. True or false?

TOUGH TO TACKLE...

3. In their eighth World Cup finals appearance Scotland were knocked out after three games. How many times have Scotland made it past the first round?

4. Italy went out in the quarter-finals after losing on penalties. They probably didn't fancy their chances – they also went out on penalties in 1994 and 1990. True or false?

5. France won the final 3-0 against Brazil but were reduced to 10 men. Which player was shown a red card?
   a) Fabien Barthez
   b) Marcel Desailly
   c) Emmanuel Petit
   d) Patrick Vieira

Japan and South Korea '02 Quick Quiz

WINNERS BRAZIL

1. Which of these teams didn't make their first World Cup finals appearance in 2002?
   a) China
   b) Ecuador
   c) Jamaica
   d) Senegal

2. The Golden Goal rule was used for the first time in 2002, meaning the first team to score in extra time would win the match. True or false?

TOUGH TO TACKLE...

3. How many goals did 1998 World Cup winners France score at the 2002 finals?

4. Which of the co-hosts went further in the competition – Japan or South Korea?

5. How many goals – not including penalty shoot-outs – were scored at the 2002 finals?
   a) 142
   b) 161
   c) 185
   d) 209

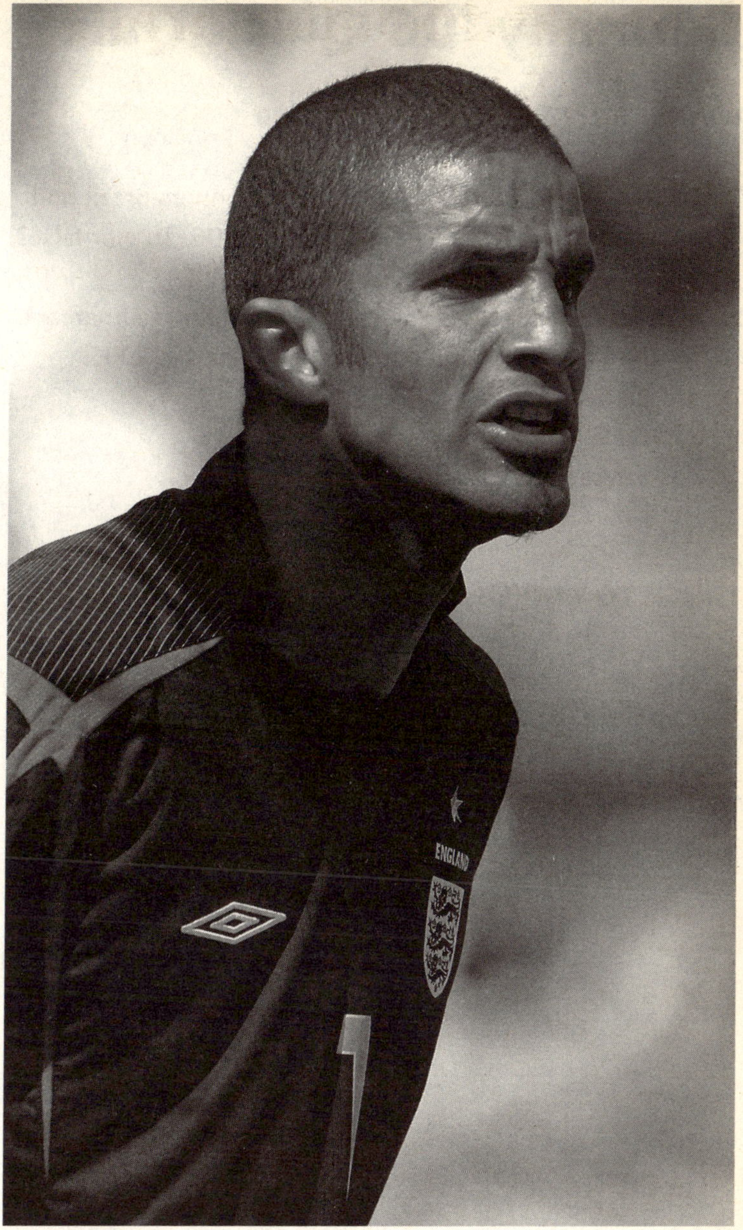
ENGLAND

Germany '06 Quick Quiz

WINNERS ?????????

1. Hosts Germany and 2002 World Cup winners Brazil both automatically qualified to compete in 2006. True or false?

2. Which of these teams entered the qualifying tournament for the first time, hoping to reach the finals in 2006?
   a) Barbados
   b) Cook Islands
   c) Latvia
   d) New Caledonia

TOUGH TO TACKLE....

3. How many teams will be playing in the 2006 World Cup finals?

4. The tournament will take place in 12 stadiums. Which ground can seat the most fans?
   a) Olympiastadion, Berlin
   b) Waldstadion, Frankfurt
   c) Stadion München, Munich
   d) Frankenstadion, Nuremberg

5. The finals begin on Friday 9th June 2006. When is the World Cup final scheduled to take place?
   a) Saturday 1st July
   b) Sunday 9th July
   c) Saturday 15th July
   d) Sunday 23rd July

All the answers

Can you kick it as a football expert? Now it's time to find out...

CUP CLASSICS
1. c. Brazil were the winners in 1958, 1962, 1970, 1994 and 2002
2. It's false – Brazil have appeared in every tournament. No wonder they've won it so many times!
3. b. Kocsis and Müller scored their hat tricks in consecutive matches too!
4. Six times – Uruguay (1930), Italy (1934), England (1966), West Germany (1974), Argentina (1978) and France (1998)
5. False – there were no tournaments in 1942 and 1946 because of the Second World War
6. d. West Germany lost the final in 1966, 1982 and 1986 – Germany also lost in 2002. Argentina, Brazil and Italy have all been runners-up twice
7. c. France '98 saw a record-breaking 171 goals. Next best was Japan and South Korea with 161
8. True – Uruguay, Italy, West Germany, Brazil, England, Argentina and France are the only winners up to and including 2002
9. c. Lafleur designed the original trophy that was given to Brazil in 1970. Gazzarriga designed the trophy that is still used today
10. They all played for the Allies team in the movie Escape To Victory. Sylvester Stallone and Michael Caine were in the side too!

BOOT-IFUL GOALS

Eusebio	– nine goals	– Portugal	– 1966
Mario Kempes	– six goals	– Argentina	– 1978
Sándor Kocsis	– 11 goals	– Hungary	– 1954
Leonidas	– eight goals	– Brazil	– 1938
Gary Lineker	– six goals	– England	– 1986
Davor Suker	– six goals	– Croatia	– 1998

URUGUAY '30 QUICK QUIZ
1. a.
2. .. It's true
3. b. The king also helped the players get time off work!
4. .. c.
5. France. Lucien Laurent was the scorer and France beat Mexico 4-1

ITALY '34 QUICK QUIZ
1. b. They lost to the USA in Rome
2. True – it's the only time that the host nation has had to qualify for the World Cup
3. b. The first match had been so tough that four Italians and six Spaniards who played in the first game didn't play in the second
4. Uruguay didn't compete – partly because they were miffed that so few European teams took part in 1930! They are the only champions in the history of the World Cup not to defend their title
5. c. The other three teams didn't make it past the first round

MYSTERY MANAGER
Franz Beckenbauer

FIND THE BALL

The ball was in square E5

FRANCE '38 QUICK QUIZ
1. Cuba played no qualifying games because all the other teams withdrew!
2. d. The final score was Brazil 6 Poland 5.
3. d. The referee insisted he put them back on!
4. b. The best Austrian players were even made to join the German team.
5. False. Only two players were in both teams.

BRAZIL '50 QUICK QUIZ
1. a. Although two places were on offer, only England, who

won the qualifying group, went.
2. It's true. Because of late withdrawals, two groups had four teams, one group had three teams and the final group included just Bolivia and Uruguay.
3. c. The record still stands today.
4. It's true. Instead four teams, Brazil, Spain, Sweden and Uruguay, went into a final league. Luckily for fans, the final league game was also the deciding match.
5. Brazil – they scored 22 goals in six games.

SWITZERLAND '54 QUICK QUIZ
1. c. Not surprisingly, this bizarre idea was ditched for the 1958 tournament!
2. b.
3. It's false. But the Uruguay players were so excited that they ran to congratulate Hohberg and accidentally knocked him unconscious!
4. d. Uruguay were beaten 2-4 by Hungary after winning the competition in 1930 and 1950 and not taking part in 1934 and 1938.
5. Hungary!

HOST NATIONS
Across
1. SWEDEN
2. USA
4. SWITZERLAND
5. WEST GERMANY
7. BRAZIL
8. ENGLAND
11. MEXICO
13. ITALY
14. JAPAN
15. GERMANY

Down
1. SOUTH KOREA
3. FRANCE
6. SPAIN
9. ARGENTINA
10. URUGUAY
12. CHILE

FACE OFF!
The players are John Terry and Gary Neville.

SWEDEN '58 QUICK QUIZ
1. True.
2. d. Wales failed to qualify in the Europe games. But after many teams withdrew in the Asia/Africa group, Wales won a ballot to play Israel, who had been given a walk-over in the final round when Sudan dropped out. Wales won 4-0 over two legs to qualify.
3. False. Three groups were settled by play-off games but both France and Yugoslavia in Group Two went through to the quarter-finals without having to play an extra game.
4. d. His tally included a hat trick against France.
5. England, who held them to a 0-0 draw.

CHILE '62 QUICK QUIZ
1. a.
2. c. He had to be persuaded by Italian officials and a group of policemen!
3. False – Bulgaria drew with England. Switzerland were the only team to lose all three games.
4. a.
5. Six players each scored four goals – Garrincha, Valentin Ivanov, Leonel Sanchez, Florian Albert, Vava and Drazen Jerkovic.

ENGLAND '66 QUICK QUIZ
1. b. Portugal and Hungary qualified from their group instead.
2. d. Wembley Stadium and White City were used for games

in London.
3. It's true. The referee missed the foul and Nobby was cautioned by a FIFA official who had watched the game in the stands.
4. c.
5. Three – one in the semi-final and two in the final!

MASCOT MANIA

A - 5   E - 6   I - 3
B - 11   F - 4   J - 8
C - 2   G - 10   K - 7
D - 9   H - 1

FINAL FOES

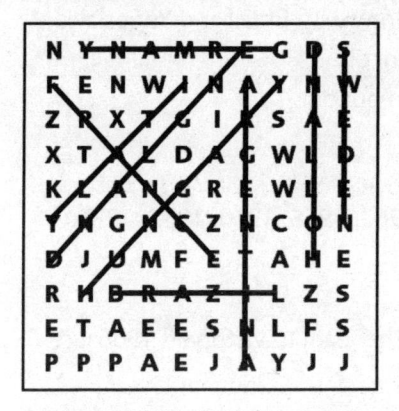

```
N Y N A M R E G D S
R E N W I N A Y M W
Z R X T G I A S A E
X T X L D A G W L D
K L A N G R E W L E
Y N G N E Z N C O N
D J U M F E T A H E
R M B R A Z I L Z S
E T A E E S N L F S
P P P A E J A Y J J
```

MEXICO '70 QUICK QUIZ

1. c.
2. Amazingly, it's true. Before 1970, injured players had to limp on to the end of the game!
3. d.
4. He became the first player to score in three first round

matches, the quarter-final, the semi-final and the final at one World Cup finals tournament. He notched up two against Czechoslovakia and one goal in each of the other five games. Uruguay's Alcide Ghiggia also scored in every match in the 1950 World Cup but Uruguay only had to play four games.

5.a. The famous trophy was stolen in 1984 and has probably been melted down.

WEST GERMANY '74 QUICK QUIZ
1. b. China would have to wait until 2002.
2. False. The cards were introduced in 1970 – the idea of an ex-referee called Ken Aston.
3. East Germany won 1-0.
4. d. Scotland beat Zaire and drew with Brazil and Yugoslavia but went out on goal difference!
5. The corner flags hadn't been put out.

ENGLAND EXPECTS...
1. 11 – in 1950, 1954, 1958, 1962, 1966, 1970, 1982, 1986, 1990, 1998 and 2002.
2. b.
3. b. Alf Ramsey – and he led the team to victory in 1966 just as he predicted!
4. It's false – England won the tournament in 1966 and so qualified automatically for 1970.
5. c. Kevin Keegan played against Spain in 1982.
6. c.
7. True. They finished second in their second round group and only the teams that finished first reached the semi-finals.

8. c.
9. d. Owen scored twice and the others notched up one goal each.
10. Argentina – England have played them five times so far. The games took place in 1962, 1966, 1986, 1998 and 2002.

SQUAD SHAKE-UP
1. Wayne Rooney
2. Rio Ferdinand
3. Ashley Cole
4. Sol Campbell
5. Steven Gerrard
6. Frank Lampard
7. Owen Hargreaves
8. Jermaine Jenas
9. Paul Robinson
10. Michael Owen

'66 HEROES

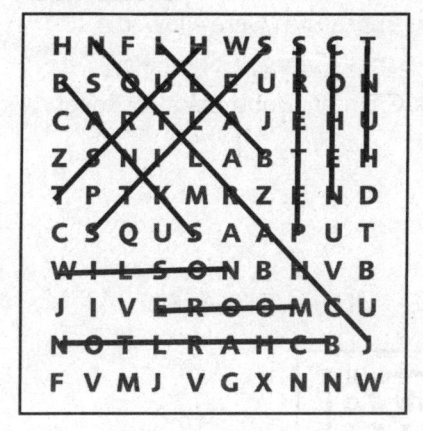

```
H N F L H W S S C T
B S Q U E U R O N
C A R T L A J E H U
Z S N I L A B T E H
T P T K M R Z E N D
C S Q U S A A P U T
W I L S O N B H V B
J I V E R O O M G U
N O T L R A H C B J
F V M J V G X N N W
```

FORWARD THINKING
Gary Lineker

HE SHOOTS...
Brazil '50 – Wilf Mannion
Switzerland '54 – Nat Lofthouse
Sweden '58 – Derek Kevan
Chile '62 – Jimmy Greaves
England '66 – Roger Hunt
Mexico '70 – Alan Mullery
Spain '82 – Bryan Robson
Mexico '86 – Peter Beardsley
Italy '90 – David Platt
France '98 – Alan Shearer
Japan and South Korea '02 – Emile Heskey

MEMORABLE MUG

From top to bottom, the three players are Jermaine Defoe, Paul Robinson and Wes Brown.

SUMMER OF '66

1. d. England drew with Uruguay 0-0.
2. a. Bobby Charlton scored in the 2-0 victory over Mexico.
3. False – he appeared in the quarter-final and semi-final too.
4. Eight – and this was before substitutes were allowed! The players were Gordon Banks, George Cohen, Ray Wilson, Nobby Stiles, Jack Charlton, Bobby Moore, Roger Hunt and Bobby Charlton.
5. It's true!

NEW KING COLE

KING – WING – WINE – VINE – VILE – VOLE – COLE

CAPTAIN MARVELS

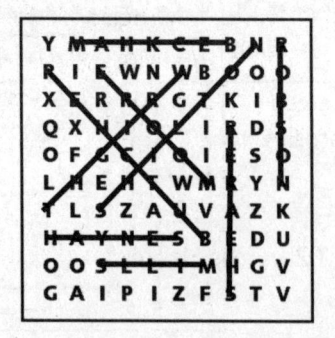

```
Y M A H K C E B N R
R I E W N W B O O
X E R R R G Z K I B
Q X H T O L I R D S
O F G T G I E S O
L H E H T W M R Y N
I L S Z A U V A Z K
H A Y N E S B E D U
O O S L L I M H G V
G A I P I Z F S T V
```

MISSING MEN
The four players are Rio Ferdinand, Gary Neville, David Beckham and Wayne Rooney.

CHARLTONS ATHLETIC
Jack Charlton – 1, 2, 5, 8 and 9
Bobby Charlton – 3, 4, 6, 7 and 10

GET THE BALLS ROLLING
Ball D is the real one.

CLASSIC CONFUSION
1. Stanley Matthews
2. Bobby Charlton
3. Bobby Moore
4. Trevor Francis
5. Peter Shilton
6. Gary Lineker
7. Paul Gascoigne
8. Alan Shearer
9. David Seaman
10. Paul Scholes

NEARLY IN '90
1. 0 – Peter Shilton kept six clean sheets.
2. c.
3. c. He scored four goals
4. False. It was Paul Gascoigne who received the yellow and famously shed a few tears.
5. b.

STAR SEARCH

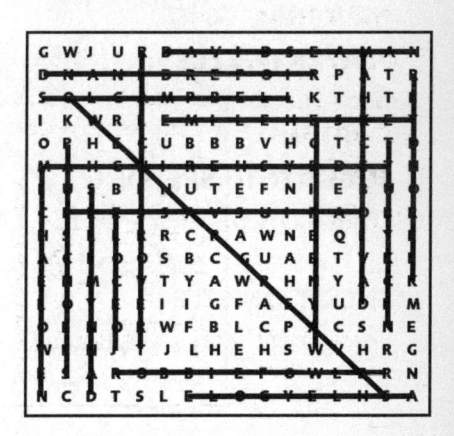

PERFECT DEFENDER
From top to bottom, the three players are John Terry, Ashley Cole and Steven Gerrard.

CAN WE HAVE OUR BALL BACK? It was in square C5.

KEEPER CONUNDRUM
Gordon Banks – 1, 5 and 6
Peter Shilton – 2, 4 and 8
David Seaman – 3, 7 and 9

PLAYER PUZZLE
Geoff Hurst.

SUBSTITUTE SPELLING
DYER – DYES – EYES – EWES – OWES – OWEN.

SHOOT ON SITE
Darren Bent scores with Route C.

QUALIFICATION QUIZ
1. Frank Lampard.
2. d.
3. a. Azerbaijan and Northern Ireland completed the group
4. d. Cole, Owen and Lampard each scored one and the fourth was an own goal.
5. It's false. Four of the games were at Old Trafford but the fifth was at Newcastle United's St James' Park.

SQUAD SQUARES
1. Wayne Rooney
2. Michael Owen
3. Paul Robinson
4. John Terry
5. Ashley Cole
6. Frank Lampard
7. Rio Ferdinand
8. Jermain Defoe
9. Joe Cole
10. Ledley King
11. Kieron Dyer
12. Gary Neville
13. Steven Gerrard
14. David Beckham

SPOT THE DIFFERENCE

THREE... TWO... ONE
1. World Cup finals debut at France '98 – David Beckham, Sol Campbell, Gary Neville, and Michael Owen.
2. World Cup finals debut at Japan and South Korea '02 – Ashley Cole, Joe Cole, Rio Ferdinand, and Owen Hargreaves.
3. Haven't yet appeared in a World Cup finals game – Steven Gerrard, Frank Lampard, Paul Robinson and John Terry.

ARGENTINA '78 QUICK QUIZ
1. It's true – 106 countries fought it out for the 16 places.
2. d. In 1962, Chile beat Switzerland 3-1
3. c. The match ended 1-1. Referee Clive Thomas blew the whistle when the ball was in the air and was mobbed by the Brazilian players.
4. b. That's what the ref claimed but some spectators said that poor Nanninga wasn't the culprit anyway!
5. Six – the same number they had managed in their previous five games put together!

SPAIN '82 QUICK QUIZ
1. c.
2. Three points – two for a win and one for a draw. It wasn't until the 1994 World Cup that three points were awarded for a win.
3. It's false. Northern Ireland won the group after beating Spain and drawing with Yugoslavia and Honduras. They only conceded one goal.
4. d. It was Hungary, who still failed to qualify for the second round!

5. d. This semi-final ended 3-3 after extra time and West Germany won 5-4 on penalties.

RECORD BREAKERS

A Youngest player – Norman Whiteside was aged just 17 years and 41 days when he played against Yugoslavia on 17th June 1982.

B Oldest player – Roger Milla was 42 years and 39 days old when he played against Russia on 28th June 1994.

C Youngest scorer – Pelé scored against Wales on 19th June 1958, when he was 17 years and 239 days old.

D Oldest scorer – Roger Milla again. He scored Cameroon's only goal against Russia.

E Most appearances in finals – Two players have each appeared in five finals. They are Antonio Carbajal (1950, 1954, 1958, 1962 and 1966) and Lothar Matthäus (1982, 1986, 1990, 1994 and 1998)

F Fastest goal – Hakan Sukur scored against South Korea in 11 seconds on 29th June 2002.

G Fastest red card – Sergio Batista was sent off after just 56 seconds against Scotland on 13th June 1986.

H Most goals scored in one tournament – Just Fontaine scored 13 goals at Sweden in 1958.

I Most goals scored from all tournaments – Gerd Müller notched up 14 World Cup finals goals. He scored 10 in 1970 in Mexico and four in West Germany in 1974.

J Most clean sheets – Peter Shilton kept 10 clean sheets in 17 games between 1982 and 1990.

MEXICO '86 QUICK QUIZ
1. a.
2. d.
3. It's false. The group was given the nickname because during the first four matches, only two goals had been scored!
4. 16 – only eight had been eliminated.
5. Three – Brazil v France, West Germany v Mexico and Belgium v Spain.

ITALY '90 QUICK QUIZ
1. d.
2. b. The real score was Republic of Ireland 0 Egypt 0!
3. Mexico 1970, when Argentina failed to qualify for the finals!
4. It's true.
5. False – he was the second player. Team-mate Pedro Monzon had been sent off 22 minutes earlier in the same game!

USA '94 QUICK QUIZ
1. a. It was the first time no UK team had appeared since 1950 when England became the first British team to take part in the finals.
2. a. Russia's Oleg Salenko scored five as his team won the match 6-1.
3. 17 – they defeated Greece 4-0 to claim their win
4. It's false – Campos claimed he'd designed the technicolour monstrosity himself!
5. True – Brazil won 3-2 on penalties.

ALL CHANGE

STAR STRIKER
Pelé

FRANCE '98 QUICK QUIZ
1. d. Spain finished third behind Nigeria and Paraguay
2. It's false – they did lose all their matches but the USA also failed to collect any points in the first round.
3. Unlucky Scotland have never made it past the first round, sometimes just missing out on goal difference.
4. True.
5. b.

JAPAN AND SOUTH KOREA '02 QUICK QUIZ
1. c. Jamaica made their first and so far only appearance in 1998.
2. It's false. The Golden Goal rule was introduced at France '98.
3. France didn't score any goals and were eliminated in the first round.

4. South Korea – they finished fourth, losing to Turkey in the third place play-off. Japan lost in the second round – to Turkey again!
5. b.

GERMANY '06 QUICK QUIZ
1. It's false. A rule change meant that Brazil didn't receive a place and had to enter the qualifying tournament. Germany, however, did automatically qualify.
2. d. The other three teams have all tried to qualify for previous tournaments.
3. 32 – the same number as in 1998 and 2002.
4. a. Berlin can seat 76,000 fans, compared to 48,000 in Frankfurt, 66,000 in Munich and 45,500 in Nuremberg.
5. b.